A TRAVEL GUIDE TO

Ancient
Rome

Other books in the Travel Guide series:

A TRAVEL GUIDE TO

Ancient
Rome

Don Nardo

**LUCENT
BOOKS®**

THOMSON
★
GALE

San Diego • Detroit • New York • San Francisco • Cleveland • New Haven, Conn. • Waterville, Maine • London • Munich

LIBRARY OF CONGRESS CATALOGING-IN-PUBLICATION DATA

Nardo, Don, 1947–
    Ancient Rome / by Don Nardo.
        p. cm. — (The traveler's guide to:)
Includes bibliographical references and index.
Summary: Examines the people, educational system, scientific and artistic discoveries,
social structure, shopping, festivals, and famous artists of Rome in 143 A.D.
    ISBN 1-59018-143-3 (lib. : alk. paper)
    1. Rome—History—Juvenile literature. 2. Rome—Guidebooks—Juvenile literature. [1.
Rome—History—Antonines, 96–192.] I. Title. II. Series.
    DG211.N37 2003
    937—dc21

                                                                            2001007505

Printed in the United States of America

Contents

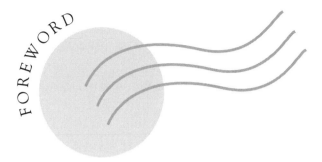

T ravel can be a unique way to learn about oneself and other cultures. The esteemed American writer and historian, John Hope Franklin, poetically expressed his conviction in the value of travel by urging, "We must go beyond textbooks, go out into the bypaths and untrodden depths of the wilderness and travel and explore and tell the world the glories of our journey." The message communicated by this eloquent entreaty is clear: The value of travel is to temper one's imagination about a place and its people with reality, and instead of thinking how things may be, to be able to experience them as they really are.

Franklin's voice is not alone in his summons for students to "travel and explore." He is joined by a stentorian chorus of thinkers that includes former president John F. Kennedy, who established the Peace Corps to facilitate cross-cultural understandings between Americans and citizens of other lands. Ideas about the benefits of travel do not spring only from contemporary times. The ancient Greek historian Herodotus journeyed to foreign lands for the purpose of immersing himself in unfamiliar cultural traditions. In this way, he believed, he might gain a firsthand understanding of people and ways of life in other places.

The joys, insights, and satisfaction that travelers derive from their journeys are not limited to cultural understanding. Travel has the added value of enhancing the traveler's inner self by expanding his or her range of experiences. Writer Paul Tournier concurs that, "The real meaning of travel, like that of a conversation by the fireside, is the discovery of oneself through contact with other people."

The Lucent Books' Travel Guide series enlivens history by introducing a new and innovative style and format. Each volume in the series presents the history of a preeminent historical travel destination written in the casual style and format of a travel guide. Whether providing a tour of fifth-century B.C. Athens, Renaissance Florence, or Shakespeare's London, each book describes a city or area at its cultural peak and orients readers to only those places and activities that are known to have existed at that time.

A high level of authenticity is achieved in the Travel Guide series. Each book is written in the present tense and addresses the reader as a prospective foreign traveler. The sense of authenticity is further achieved, whenever possible, by the inclusion of descriptive quotations by contemporary writers who knew the place; information on fascinating historical sites; and travel tips meant to explain unusual cultural idiosyncrasies that give depth and texture to all great cultural centers. Even shopping details, such as where to buy an ermine, trimmed gown or a much-needed house slave, are included to inform readers of what items were sought after throughout history.

Looked at collectively, this series presents an appealing presentation of many of the cultural and social highlights of Western civilization. The collection also provides a framework for discussion about the larger historical currents that dominated not only each travel destination but countries and entire continents as well. Each book is customized by the author to bring to the fore the most important and most interesting characteristics that define each title. High standards of scholarship are assured in the series by the generous peppering of relevant quotes and extensive bibliographies. These tools provide readers a scholastic standard for their own research as well as a guide to direct them to other books, periodicals, and websites that will provide them greater breadth and detail.

A Note to the Reader

I n this book, various aspects of ancient Roman history, society, and government, as well as art, architecture, and other cultural elements are examined in the format of a modern travel guide. On the one hand, this approach provides an innovative and entertaining way to learn about ancient Roman life and ideas. On the other, it presents some technical problems that do not exist in straightforward history texts.

The most prominent of these problems is that a number of accepted conventions of dating, measurement, and so forth have changed over the centuries. Today, for example, most history books automatically use B.C. meaning "before Christ" and A.D., denoting the Christian era. In the standard B.C.-A.D. scheme, the date for Rome's founding, an event described in this volume, is 753 B.C., or 753 years before the beginning of the Christian era.

The difficulty is that the B.C.-A.D. dating system did not exist in ancient times;

Christian scholars introduced it in the early Middle Ages. The ancient Romans had a number of different dating systems of their own, which often existed side by side. It stands to reason, therefore, that if this travel guide had actually been written in ancient times, the author would have used one of the dating systems then in vogue. However, using such an obscure and unfamiliar system in a modern book would not be very practical; so for the sake of clarity and convenience, this book uses the standard B.C.-A.D. dating system.

Another concern is the dating of the travel guide itself. The author has chosen the year A.D. 143, five years into the reign of Antoninus Pius, the fourth of the so-called five good emperors. During his reign Rome was, more or less, at the height of its power and influence and had not yet begun its long slide into oblivion, the famous decline and fall. Roman society may also have been most prosperous, happy, and optimistic in this era. The year in question is the approximate date for the *Roman Panegyric*, a speech in which noted Greek writer Aelius Aristides heaped praises on Rome for bringing civilization and prosperity to the known world. Prosperity always encourages tourism. As the capital of the vast Empire, the city of Rome had long been a popular destination for traders, tourists, and other travelers from across the Mediterranean world and beyond. One can safely assume that during Antoninus's reign, an age of peace and security, the volume of such visitors was as large as it would ever be.

In the same way that the Romans had their own dating systems, they had their own units of measurement. But as in the case of dates, this book employs modern units of measurement—miles and square miles—as well as degrees of temperature and so forth, to make the text more understandable to modern readers. Except for these conventions, all aspects of this travel guide are authentic. They are based on evidence derived from surviving ancient literary texts and studies made by archaeologists and other scholars of paintings, sculptures, buildings, tools, weapons, coins, and other ancient artifacts. All of the places and sites described are or were real; and many still exist in modern Rome and its environs, although they are now in a ruined state.

CHAPTER ONE

A Brief History of Rome

For travelers and traders from across the known world, all roads do indeed lead to Rome. From its lofty vantage on a series of low hills along a bend in the Tiber River a few miles inland from the western Italian coast, Rome stands as the capital and greatest city of the mightiest realm in human history. People everywhere look to the city and its leaders as the source of political guidance, social and communal amenities, physical security, and the rule of law that ensures justice for all citizens of the empire. And they marvel at how one great city has helped to establish or to expand and improve so many others. The Greek writer Aelius Aristides recently summed up Rome's achievement this way:

Were there ever so many cities, inland and maritime? Were they ever so thoroughly modernized? Could a person in the past travel thus, counting up the cities by the number of days on the road? . . . Every place is full of gymnasia, fountains, gateways, temples, shops, and schools. . . . Gifts never stop flowing from you to the cities . . . [which] shine in radiance and beauty. . . . Only those outside your Empire, if there are any, are fit to be pitied for losing such blessings. . . . Greek and [non-Greek] can now readily go wherever they please with their property or without it. . . . You have surveyed the whole world, built bridges of all sorts across rivers, cut down mountains to make paths for chariots, filled the deserts with hostels, and civilized it all with system and order.[1]

People also view Rome as a venerable storehouse of cultural tradition and marvelous monuments, many dating from past ages, as well as the site of numerous famous historical events. It was there, for example, where the brave Horatius single-handedly held off an Etruscan army while

10

kitchen, a dining room (equipped with heating ducts under the floor), and several bedrooms on the second story.

A few roadside country inns are larger and more elaborate, but still offer the same basic services, as do the inns in the towns located along or near the major roads. There are certain advantages to staying in a town, however, as opposed to an isolated country inn. For example, all Roman towns of at least moderate size have public baths, many of which feature hot and cold pools in which to relax. Such establishments also have snack bars, exercise and massage rooms, and often libraries and reading rooms. There are also several different kinds of eating places, from simple snack bars that sell fast food to more elegant places with multiple dining rooms.

Whether in town or along open stretches of road, travelers who cannot afford or for some reason do not want to stay at inns can avail themselves of private lodgings. Owners of private houses rent out rooms, which are as a rule less expensive than the ones at the inns. Owners usually hang out signs or plaques to advertise and these can be quite clever, as in the following example: "If you're clean and neat, then there's a house ready and waiting for you. If you're dirty—well, I'm ashamed to say it, but you're welcome too."[11]

When it comes to finding an inn or guest house along the roads to Rome, one can, of course, simply take one's chances and stop at the nearest one. For those travelers who prefer to plan ahead, maps

This sketch shows a well-to-do country home not far from Rome.

and guide books are available. Such road books (*itineraria*[12]) list the towns, inns, stables, major sites, and other notable places along a given road or route. A few more elaborate maps are available, though they are very expensive and only the well-to-do can afford copies. These feature not only little numbers indicating the distances between towns, inns, and other stopping places, but also little picture-symbols advising the traveler about the quality of the facilities offered. A picture of a four-sided building with a courtyard in the middle, for example, indicates an inn with excellent facilities. A picture showing a house with a twin-peaked roof, on the other hand, indicates a country inn of average quality.

Once inside the city of Rome, travelers will find many inns, although most of these lack courtyards, a common feature of the roadside facilities. The city inns also tend to have smaller, more cramped rooms, many with no windows. A few establishments supply candles or oil lamps, but many do not; so the traveler is advised to carry one or the other to avoid the obvious inconveniences of a pitch-black cubicle.

Snack Bars and Restaurants

Once settled into a room in the city, the traveler will no doubt be concerned about finding a good meal. This presents no problem, because Roman cities, including the capital itself, are replete with eating

A family eats out at one of the many snack bars found in the capital city. The proprietor is cooking fish on a grill while another customer examines his fruit.

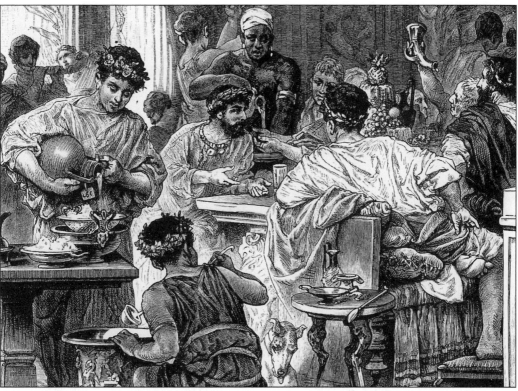

Private dinner parties like this one are common in upper-class Roman households. Servants pour and serve wine to the host's guests, some of whom recline while eating.

establishments of all kinds. If one is looking for something fast and simple, there are hundreds of snack bars (*thermopolii*), at least one or two in every city block. (Even more can be found near city gates, bathhouses, and the main Forum.) These small cookshops each typically have a marble-topped counter opening onto the sidewalk. Customers walk up to the counter and order, after which they can either stand there and eat or take the food back to their rooms. The cooking is done on a metal grill over a small charcoal furnace recessed into the counter. Recently cooked food, such as sausages and other

grilled meats, stays warm in ceramic jars. Bread, cheese, figs, dates, nuts, cakes, and of course wine are also available.

If the visitor is looking for a sit-down meal, he or she should look for a regular restaurant (*popina* or *taberna*). Most such establishments have streetside counters like the snack bars, but also feature one or more small dining rooms equipped with tables and chairs. A few more elaborate versions have private dining rooms, latrines, and also couches around the tables for those who prefer to recline, rather than sit, while eating. Some *popinae* furnish entertainment as well, including

A well-to-do family enjoys a sumptuous meal while some acrobats enter (at left) to entertain. Most Romans cannot afford such luxury.

musicians, dancing girls, and occasionally jugglers and other specialty acts.

As for the fare available in such restaurants, a wide range of foods and prepared dishes are available. In Rome, breakfast (*ientaculum*) is usually a light meal consisting of bread or wheat biscuits, either dipped in wine or covered with honey, sometimes along with a little cheese or some olives and/or raisins. Foreigners who may be used to heartier breakfasts can order extra bread or some kind of meat. In the early afternoon, many Romans take a light lunch (*prandium*). It usually consists of cold foods such as bread, salads, and fruits; but once again, local restaurant owners are always happy to supply foreign visitors with extra courses.

The main meal of the day (*cena*) can be simple or elaborate, depending on what the customer prefers or can afford. In better restaurants, supper is customarily served in three courses, collectively called *ab ovo usque ad malla* ("from the egg to the apples"). The first course, *gustatio*, features appetizers such as salads, mushrooms and other raw vegetables, oysters, eggs, and sardines. The second and main course, *prima mensa*, normally consists of cooked vegetables and meats. These include poultry, fish, lamb, wild boar, and pork, the Romans' favorite meat. (More exotic dishes, such as lobster, pheasant, ostrich, peacocks and peacock brains, flamingo tongues, and fish livers, are not available at restaurants; because of their great cost, such items are usually found only at ban-

quets given in upper-class homes.) The third course, dessert (*secunda mensa*), most often consists of fruits, nuts, and/or honey cakes and other pastries.

Spices help to make these foods more appetizing. Because Rome attracts traders from all parts of the known world, a wide variety of spices is available in the capital. Only a partial list includes salt, pepper, ginger, cinnamon, balsam, sweet marjoram, myrrh, cassia, frankincense, rue, mint, and parsley. Some of these are used to make tangy sauces, one of the most popular being a salty fish sauce called *garum*. By contrast, *defrutum* is a sweet sauce made by boiling fruit juice until it thickens.

Non-Romans are advised that the main drink in Rome (as well as in other parts of its realm) is wine. Following ancient custom, almost all Romans mix their wine with water in a large bowl called a *crater*, from which they ladle it into goblets. Drinking undiluted wine is seen as undignified or even uncivilized. (Drinking milk is also viewed as uncivilized.) Many people sweeten their wine with honey, producing a popular drink called *mulsum*, while lower-class people often drink *posca*, a mixture of water and a low-quality, vinegar-like wine. Beer is popular mainly in the northern provinces, but a few taverns in the capital do carry it. By now it should be clear that when it comes to lodging and food, Rome has a wide variety of both to suit the needs and pocketbooks of everyone.

CHAPTER FOUR

Markets and Shopping

Rome is a paradise for shoppers. And many of the tourists who visit the city each year spend a great deal of their hard-earned money buying food, clothes, jewelry, glassware, pottery, metal wares, and more. That Roman markets have so much to offer should come as no surprise. The imperial capital lies at the center of a vast trading network that stretches across the Mediterranean world and far beyond.

The incredible diversity of foreign goods that flow steadily into the Roman heartland and its capital is illustrated by a mere partial list of typical Italian imports: wheat from Egypt and North Africa; also from Africa, spices, wild animals for the public games, oil for lamps, and ivory and citrus wood for making and decorating fine furniture; from Spain and Gaul, copper pots and pans, pottery dishes, and fine wines; also from Spain, gold, silver, tin, and horses; from Syria, glassware and fine textiles; from Britain, tin, lead, silver, cat-

tle, and oysters; wool from the coasts of Asia Minor; linen and papyrus parchment from Egypt; from Greece, honey for sweetening foods and magnificent statues and paintings; from the Greek islands, fuller's earth for finishing and cleaning clothes; spices, perfumes, and precious stones from faraway India; and silk and spices from even more distant China. Amazed at this rich variety of goods from so many diverse provinces and countries, Aelius Aristides recently remarked:

If one would look at all these things, he must needs behold them either by visiting the entire civilized world or by coming to this city. . . . Here the merchant vessels come carrying these many products from all regions in every season . . . so that the city appears a kind of supermarket of the world . . . so there is a common channel to Rome and all [markets and industries] meet here: trade, shipping, agriculture, metallurgy [and] all the arts and crafts that are or ever have been. . . . And whatever one does not see here neither did nor does exist.[13]

Getting the Goods to Market

Traders and merchants are well aware, of course, how such a wide diversity of products make it to Rome's markets. But ordinary tourists are not always so well-informed, so a brief overview of the process follows. First, traders rarely use Rome's extensive road system to carry bulky items long distances. Overland transport is too slow and consequently very expensive, and the heavier the items being transported, the more the cost.

Long-range trade is more often accomplished, therefore, by taking advantage of liquid highways—the seas and Tiber River. The cargo ships are typically wooden sailing vessels. Their hulls are covered with

Some of the goods this Roman merchant offers at his modest shop come from central Italy, but many are imported from distant and exotic places.

Most cargo ships are relatively small vessels with a single mast. This huge ship, a converted war galley, carries loads of grain and other unusually heavy cargoes.

pitch[14] to keep them watertight, and they are painted with a mixture of soft wax and colored pigments. An average cargo ship is about 60 to 100 feet long, 17 to 30 feet wide, and carries cargoes ranging from 50 to 250 tons. A few cargo vessels, notably those that ferry grain from Egypt to Rome for distribution to the urban masses or that lug heavy stone artifacts, are much larger. (In A.D. 40, the emperor Caligula had a stone obelisk shipped to the capital from Egypt in a boat specially built to carry a burden of thirteen hundred tons.)

Exchanging Currency

Before the traveler actually begins shopping in Rome, it is imperative to make sure he or she has the proper currency to pay for goods. Most merchants and shopkeepers prefer standard Roman coins, such as the *denarius*, the *sestertius* (worth one-quarter of a *denarius*), and the *as* (worth one-quarter of a *sestertius*). Visitors with less accepted local currencies (such as Greek, Syrian, or Persian), bronze ingots, jewelry, or other valuable goods will need to exchange them for more acceptable Roman coins.

Exchanging currency is the work of Roman bankers, called *argentarii* (singular *argentarius*). They are typically private businessmen, most of them non-noblemen, including some freed slaves, since members of the noble patrician class usually consider dealing with money to be beneath their dignity. Moneychangers often set up their tables (*mensa publica*) outside temples, on street corners, and at various points in marketplaces. They carefully weigh all coins and other valuables and are very adept at spotting phony gold and silver coins. The going commission rate they charge for their services is about 6 percent. Bankers also provide other financial services, such as lending money (at rates of 6 to 10 percent); taking money and other valuables on deposit; buying, selling, and managing land and buildings; and collecting outstanding debts.

Having secured the proper coinage, the visitor is ready to begin shopping. Shops and vendors of various kinds can be found all over Rome, but a good many are concentrated in certain areas, especially in or near the various fora. The city's main Forum used to be the principal marketplace, for instance. But as more and more important public buildings rose there, the merchants slowly got pushed out. The main food market became known as the Macellum, an open area lying northeast of the Forum. (Some of the merchants were pushed out again when the Temple of Peace was constructed in the area in the early 70s A.D.) As in the case of other shopping areas in various parts of the city, vendors set up their wagons, tents, or other temporary stalls in the open portion of the marketplace, while more permanent shops constructed of masonry line the outer edges of the square. Other heavy concentrations of shops can be found on the eastern slope of the Palatine Hill, in the crowded Subura, and in Trajan's Market (the elegant complex facing Trajan's Forum). Trajan's Market alone contains more than 150 separate shops.

Shopping for Clothes and Shoes

Among the more common shops in Trajan's Market and elsewhere are those that sell clothes or fabric (which wives, mothers, and slaves use to make clothes at home). The most important

Common Roman Coins

Commerce and shopping could not exist without viable coinage. Not surprisingly, then, production of Roman coins is widespread and numerous types and denominations are made from various metals. During his long reign, Augustus standardized the coinage in a new system that is still in place today. Each coin bears the head of the emperor on its obverse (front) to signify that it is genuine tender guaranteed by the government. The basic breakdown of coins in this system (ranging from most to least valuable) is the *aureus*, made of about $1/4$ ounce of gold; the silver *denarius*, worth $1/25$ of an *aureus*; the bronze (sometimes brass) *sestertius*, equal to $1/4$ of a *denarius* (and $1/100$ of an *aureus*); the brass *dupondius*, worth half of a *sestertius* (and $1/200$ of an *aureus*); the copper (sometimes bronze) *as*, worth $1/4$ of a *sestertius* (and $1/400$ of an *aureus*); the brass (sometimes bronze) *semis*, worth half an *as* (and $1/800$ of an *aureus*); and the bronze (sometimes copper) *quadrans*, valued at $1/4$ of an *as* (and $1/1,600$ of an *aureas*).

and fashionable article of outdoor clothing for men remains the toga, an oblong piece of cloth about nineteen feet long, which wraps around the body to create various folds and drapes. It is interesting to note that throughout Rome's history many people have complained about wearing the toga because, they say, it is impractical, not warm enough in winter, too warm in summer, restricts body movements, and leaves only one arm free (since the other has to support the garment's main drape). But reverence for tradition has won out. (Centuries ago, women also wore the toga for formal wear; over time, however, they adopted instead an outer cloak called the *palla*, which can be draped in many ways, including over the head, and comes in numerous colors.)

This is one of several accepted ways of wrapping a toga.

The most common garment seen in clothes shops is the simple tunic, often worn under the toga. The tunic is made from two rectangular pieces of cloth stitched up the sides, with holes cut for the head and arms. Men and women both wear it knee-length, while many woman wear an ankle-length dress, the *stola*, over it. Rich women wear *stolae* of silk or other fine materials, while ordinary women settle for linen or wool. Clothes shops also carry cloaks, capes, scarves, hoods, headbands, and hats.

For footwear, the traveler has large numbers of shoe and boot shops to choose from. The most popular item in the local Mediterranean climate, particularly in the spring and summer months, is the sandal (*crepida*), which comes in a wide variety of shapes and styles. For those visitors from cooler climates, canvas and leather shoes and boots are also sold in Rome. Very popular among Romans and non-Romans alike are soldiers' and farm workers' boots, which feature soles studded with nails for better traction.

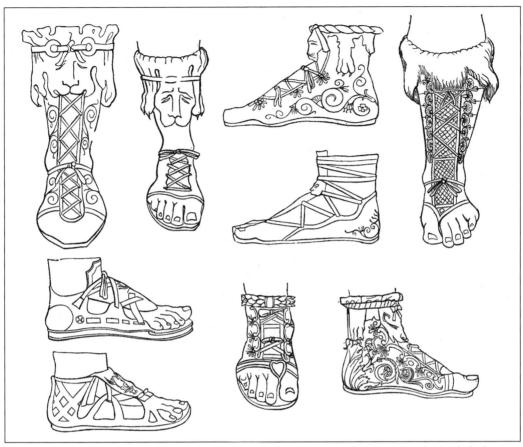

A variety of footwear is available in Rome's shops. Seen here are a leather boot (top left); cloth shoe (top center); and a number of different styles of sandal.

Gifts and Souvenirs to Take Home

Tourists, like the locals, usually buy clothes and shoes for their own use. But visitors, especially those who come to Rome from distant parts of the empire or from foreign lands, also like to purchase gifts they can take back home to family and friends. Among the most popular items in this category are grooming aids, particularly for women. These include hairbrushes, hairnets, wigs, and jars of creams, pastes, oils,

colored dyes, and perfumes. (Both male and female Romans use perfume to cover body odors. They also sometimes add a bit of perfume to their wine to sweeten the breath.) Another popular gift is the "pocket set," containing tweezers, a nail cleaner, an ear cleaner, a toothpick, a small mirror, and some basic makeup items.

For those who can afford it, jewelry makes a thoughtful gift, and jewelry shops are found all over the city of Rome. (Foreigners are sometimes surprised to

Amphorae: Essential to Commerce

Another commodity essential to commerce and shopping consists of amphorae, the large pottery jars used to transport liquids such as wine and olive oil (and occasionally solid foods such as olives, dates, and nuts). Well before Rome was a major economic power, they were in wide use by the Greeks, whose word for such a jar, *amphoreus*, the Romans adopted as amphora. There are at least forty different types and styles of amphorae, but most stand 3 to 4 feet high, have a capacity of from 6 to 20 gallons, are wide in the middle and taper to a narrow mouth, and have two vertical handles near that mouth. The inside of such a vessel is often coated with rosin, a residue from the distillation of resin from pine trees, or some other material to make it watertight; and the mouth is sealed by a stopper made of cork or fired clay. Many, if not most, amphorae are stamped or painted with inscriptions, often including the names of the owners of the estates where they were made or the merchants who transported them; the origin of the contents; the weight of said contents; and/or shipping information. On merchant ships, the jars are stacked, either upright or on their sides, in several layers. Some of the larger ships can carry several thousand amphorae at a time.

learn that most of the skilled work in these shops is performed by slaves or freedmen; and freedmen often rise to the position of manager or even owner.) The most common types of jewelry sold in Rome are gold chains, bracelets, and anklets; strings of pearls; rings with precious gems set in gold or silver; earrings of gold, silver, bronze, pearl, and/or emerald; and decorative hair pins, brooches, medallions, and cameos.

Another gift item requiring great skill and creativity to make is glassware. Although glass artifacts are manufactured in various parts of the Empire, the capital boasts a number of world-famous glass shops. Not long after the technique of glassblowing was perfected (about two hundred years ago, probably in Syria), Rome became an important center for the industry; and glass jars, bottles, bowls, and perfume flasks made in Rome remain highly prized. Among the more popular items with tourists and locals alike are those with exquisite figures and landscapes etched onto their surfaces.

Other popular gifts include tools, weapons, cooking pots, tableware, figurines, brooches, and other objects made of metals, including copper, tin, bronze (an alloy, or mixture, of copper and tin), brass (an alloy of copper and zinc), iron, lead, pewter (an alloy of lead and tin), silver, and gold. Of these, gold is of course the most precious and expensive because it is so rare. Also, people tend to horde it, taking what little there is out of circulation. One common view is that there will always be new supplies of gold discovered and mined for humanity's benefit; but a

few respected Roman scholars have struck a note of caution that must give shoppers, and indeed all of us, some pause. In his famous encyclopedia, penned about eighty years ago, Pliny the Elder warned that supplies of gold and other valuable natural materials may be limited and perhaps even threatened by human desire for them:

> What [nature] has hidden and kept underground—those things that

This set of fine silver serving ware was made during Augustus's reign. Such items make excellent gifts, but are too pricey for the average Roman shopper.

cannot be found immediately—destroy us and drive us to the depths. As a result the mind boggles at the thought of the long-term effect of draining the earth's resources and the full impact of greed. How innocent, how happy, indeed how comfortable life might be if it coveted nothing from anywhere other than the surface of the earth—in brief, nothing except what is immediately available! [15]

CHAPTER FIVE

Gods and Religious Festivals

No visitor to the Roman capital can fail to be impressed by the spirituality of the local inhabitants. As is the case in most foreign lands, near and distant, religious belief and worship is a crucial pillar of life in the city of Rome and throughout the Empire. Religious rituals, particularly sacrifice and/or prayer, accompany numerous gatherings and important endeavors, both private and public. Rome also has its local religious festivals and holidays. Most of these, along with the gods they honor and the rituals of worship attending them, are perfectly familiar to the residents of the empire; however, some basic information is provided here for the sake of Persians, Arabs, Germans, Indians, and other foreign traders and tourists who sometimes find Roman rituals confusing or odd.

A Wide Array of Accepted Gods

First, visitors from beyond Rome's borders will be relieved and pleased to know that the Romans are uniquely tolerant in religious matters. They openly accept and respect the gods of all peoples. In fact, though they started out with their own distinct pantheon—the group of gods in the so-called state religion—over the centuries the Romans came to embrace numerous foreign gods; each god has its cult (the beliefs, rites, and ceremonies constituting its worship), and the various cults coexist in harmony.

The chief god of the state pantheon is Jupiter, whom the Greeks call Zeus. His symbols are the thunderbolt and the eagle and his main temple, on the Capitoline Hill, is viewed as the heart of the state religion. Other important members of the state pantheon are Juno, Jupiter's wife and protector of women and childbirth; Minerva, goddess of war and protector of craftsmen; Mercury, Jupiter's messenger, who protects travelers and tradesmen; Apollo, the versatile deity of prophecy, music, and healing; Vesta, goddess of the

Father Jupiter brandishes his thunderbolts while riding an eagle, his symbol.

hearth; two-faced Janus, who watches over doorways; and Mars, god of war.

As for the foreign gods that Rome has come to embrace, some of which tourists will be more familiar with, the oldest and one of the most revered is Cybele, the "Great Mother," from Asia Minor, a nature and fertility goddess. From Egypt came Isis, who is widely associated with goodness and purification of sin. And from Persia came Mithras, whose followers preach treating all people with kindness and respect. The worship of Mithras is a particularly clear example of Roman

religious tolerance; the Romans and Persians have been at political and military odds off and on for centuries, yet many Romans did not hesitate to accept this deity into their hearts and homes. The god's cult is particularly popular among merchants and soldiers. They see Mithras as a bringer of light and truth who was sent to Earth to kill a sacred bull, from whose blood all living things sprang. (Because the death of the bull is thought to have taken place in a cave, the god's worshipers construct his temples underground.)

By contrast, another cult that originated in the East has failed to attract many adherents. Its members call themselves Christians, after Jesus Christ, a Jewish preacher who died about a century ago in Palestine. They claim he was sent to Earth to help humankind, as Mithras was. In fact, some Christian beliefs appear to be similar to those of Mithraism and other Eastern cults, featuring, for instance, the miraculous birth of a sacred baby, baptism, and the promise of resurrection. The Romans have no argument with the Christians' basic beliefs, therefore. Many people are appalled, however, by reports that secret Christian ceremonies may involve cannibalism and the murder of children; also, most Romans are insulted that the members of the cult refuse to accept other people's gods or to worship the emperor. The prevailing view is that such arrogance may anger the state gods and unleash their wrath on Rome. For these reasons, most Romans reject the

Christians, and for safety's sake visitors are advised to steer clear of known Christians and their houses.

Religious Festivals and Games

Coincidentally, the attempt to appease the gods is one of the main motivating factors behind the many religious festivals (*feriae*) celebrated in Rome. Almost all Romans accept that failing to celebrate a festival or celebrating in an incorrect or improper manner might provoke the ire of the god or gods involved. The festivals are also part of revered tradition and afford the populace the opportunity to share in and enjoy national holidays. In addition, a large proportion of the tourists who visit Rome each year do so to take part in the unusually large and colorful religious celebrations staged in the capital.

In these public festivals (*feriae publicae*), priests conduct rituals outside the temples while worshipers watch. Afterward, considerable feasting and merriment take place. (Foreigners should take note that

A painting captures members of a Christian sect at one of their meetings. Many Romans are suspicious of the Christians for their secrecy and refusal to accept others' gods.

another kind of celebration having a religious element is the staging of public games, or *ludi*, which are almost always held in honor of a god or gods. They are technically not *feriae*, but most people observe them in the same manner as the festivals.)

One of the most prominent of the Roman festivals, popular with both locals and tourists, is the Saturnalia, celebrated from December 17 through 23. It originated as an observance of the winter solstice and honors Saturn, the god of sowing seeds. Traditional elements include

A well-to-do Roman family celebrates the Saturnalia. During this popular holiday, it is customary for the master and his servants to exchange places.

The Great Mother Goddess

Cybele, the "Great Mother," one of the most popular deities worshiped in the Roman Empire, originated in Phrygia (in west-central Asia Minor). She is a fertility goddess whom many people believe can cure (or if angry, inflict) disease and protect people in wartime. Her male consort, Attis, is often worshiped along with her. The Romans began worshiping Cybele in 204 B.C., near the close of the Second Punic War. At this time, a Roman ambassador journeyed to Phrygia and brought her sacred black stone (which is said to have fallen from the sky) back to Rome. There, they installed it in a temple built to her on the Palatine Hill. During the first century A.D., Cybele's festival, the Megalesia, celebrated from April 4 through 10, became popular throughout the Empire.

suspending all business activities, sacrificing to the god, feasting, wearing formal clothes, gift-giving, exchanging goodwill sentiments, and lighting candles; also, in many homes masters and slaves exchange places for a day, the masters serving the slaves.[16]

Other popular festivals and celebrations that take place in the city include the Compitalia (most often held January 3 through 5), in which people observe the end of the agricultural year by erecting shrines at crossroads; the Lupercalia (February 15), which celebrates and promotes the fertility of the soil; the Megalisia (April 4 through 10), honoring Cybele; the Floralia (April 28 through May 3), the spring and flower festival of the nature goddess Flora (along with six days of games, the *ludi Florales*); the Vestalia (June 9) dedicated to Vesta; the *ludi Apollinares* (July 6 through 13), games

honoring Apollo; and the *ludi Romani* (September 5 through 19), involving the sacrifice of a cow and a sumptuous feast in honor of Jupiter. Tourists should be aware that rooms in the city are scarce during these holidays, especially the *ludi Romani*; so it is prudent to make reservations well ahead of time.

Roman Priests

Presiding over the public festivals, as well as over many aspects of private worship, are the priests. Because priests of one kind or another are extremely important members of the community in all foreign lands, many visitors to Rome are naturally inquisitive about the status and practices of Roman priests. The fact is that these men are indeed of high social status. They receive training in religious matters and then execute their religious duties on a part-time basis. Exceptions are those who

49

Priests sacrifice animals on an altar in front of the Temple of Jupiter on the Capitoline Hill. Visiting worshipers can watch or take part in this ceremony.

head the staffs of temples and are full-time officials paid by the state; but their job is to maintain the temple and its sanctuary (surrounding sacred grounds), not to guide people in spiritual matters.

In general, public priests and priestesses attempt to maintain favorable relations with the gods by leading ceremonies at large outdoor altars on behalf of the state and people as a whole. As for the priests, various kinds are organized into groups called "colleges." The highest priests of Rome's state religion are the pontiffs (*pontifices*), who belong to the most important priestly college, the *collegium pontificum*. Originally, three of

them served jointly, but today there are sixteen. Their duties are to determine the dates of religious festivals, to decide which days are acceptable for people to conduct legal business, to keep records of major events, and in general to make sure the state religion runs smoothly. The most important and prestigious among these men is the *pontifex maximus*, Rome's chief priest; after Julius Caesar and Augustus held this post, it became tradition for each Roman emperor to do so.

A more specialized high priest is the *rex sacrorum*, "king of the sacred objects." For tradition's sake (since maintaining tradition is extremely important to the

Romans), he performs certain public sacrifices that the Roman kings did before they were eliminated more than six hundred years ago. For instance, twice a year he sacrifices a ram at the Regia, a shrine said to have been erected by one of the kings.

Among the other groups of priests that are of special interest to tourists are the augurs and haruspices, who perform divination (the interpretation of divine signs by observing the behavior of birds or the entrails of sacrificial animals). The ceremonies of divination, many of which take place in public, are always colorful and visitors regularly flock to them along with the locals. Another group of priests, the *flamines*, are assigned by the state to serve particular gods. (One *flamen* each is assigned to Jupiter, Mars, Flora, Ceres, Falacer, Furrina, Palatua, Pomona, Portunus, Quirinus, Volturnus, and Vulcan.) Still another group of priests, the *fetiales*, who are chosen from aristocratic families, oversee the rituals attending foreign relations, such as making treaties and declaring war. War cannot be officially declared, for example, until one of the *fetiales* hurls a spear into enemy territory (or into an area representing such territory inside the temple of the war goddess, Bellona).

The Sacred Vestal Virgins

Besides the priests, Rome has some priestesses, usually in the cults of foreign female

During their first ten years in the priesthood, the Vestals learn to execute their duties. In this painting of a scene from their school, an older priestess instructs the novices.

The Fates: Real or Imaginary?

Many people in the Empire see these three traditional goddesses as having the power to guide human destiny. They are usually pictured in art and literature as old women spinning or weaving. The Greeks call them Klotho, Lachesis, and Atropos, while the Romans know them as Nona, Decuma, and Morta, collectively called the Parcae. Believers also differ on the methods the Fates employ. Some people think their fateful spinning leads up to and halts at the moment of birth; others hold that the spinning continues throughout life until the thread runs out. On the other hand, a number of skeptics suggest that these deities are only imaginary and that people themselves decide their own fate by their decisions and actions. Such differences of opinion are not likely to be settled any time soon.

deities such as Isis, although the state religion has an important group of female priests—the Vestal Virgins. It is beneficial to elaborate on these special, extremely sacred women because they are highly protected and reclusive, and therefore rarely seen in public. Indeed, visitors to Rome often wait hours or days to catch a fleeting glimpse of them; so it is not surprising that they are a very popular tourist attraction in and of themselves.

In very ancient days there were only two Vestal Virgins. That number eventually increased to four and today six of these priestesses serve the state religion. Their main duties are to watch over the sacred fire on the state hearth in the Temple of Vesta (in the capital), and to care for the sacred objects kept in the temple. Another duty they perform is to make a special salt cake used in various religious festivals throughout the year. The Vestals are chosen by the *pontifex maximus* from a pool of aristocratic girls aged six to ten; and once accepted, they are obliged to serve for at least thirty years. Actually, many end up serving for life.

Maintained at state expense, the Vestals dwell in a house called the Hall of Vesta, located near the main Forum, and they wear plain white linen dresses. The white both symbolizes and emphasizes their purity, for they must remain virgins throughout their service. Any of their number who is found guilty of being unchaste is buried alive and her lover is beaten to death. The Vestal Virgins have the power to grant a reprieve to a criminal if they meet him on his way to his execution; and anyone standing among the Vestals is immune from attack.

Sacrifice

The temples, religious festivals, and priests are essential to the public worship of the gods. That worship is not only a major underpinning of the Roman community, but it also provides guidance and comfort for the individual in his or her everyday life. In the Roman view, which may differ somewhat from that of some visitors, the relationship between a person and a god takes the form of a sacred contract. If a person observes the proper rituals, consisting mainly of sacrifice and prayer, the god will react favorably. On the other hand, if the person fails in his or her religious duty, the god may become angry and exact punishment. The Latin expression coined to describe this relationship is *"do ut des,"* meaning "I, the mortal, give to you, the god, so that you may give back to me."

Sacrifice, the offering of material gifts to a god, is of prime importance among the rituals of Roman worship. One very common kind of sacrifice involves the fulfillment of a vow. A person privately vows or the state publicly vows to give a god a gift if and when the god grants the request of the person or the state. Such vows are often recorded in writing. If the god does not deliver, there is no obligation to go through with the sacrifice. Sacrifices made in fulfillment of vows are known as votive offerings or *exvotos;* they range from lavish gifts, such as monuments, statues, and entire altars, to modest ones, such as figurines or coins, and bronze, silver, or gold plaques. Most often

The Temple of Vesta and Floor Plan

these offerings are deposited in temples. But according to tradition they are sometimes placed in sacred springs or deep pits. Among the other motives for sacrifice are obeying a request made by a god in a dream, seeking the favor of a god or gods, and celebrating an anniversary or a special event.

The most popular form of Roman sacrifice, the kind that tourists most often see performed in public religious festivals, involves the killing and eating of animals such as oxen, goats, sheep, and pigs. Male animals are offered up to male deities and female animals to female deities. Usually, someone leads the "victim" of an intended sacrifice to an altar and, after sprinkling salt, wine, flour, or a sacred cake over the beast's head, a priest slits its throat and cuts it up. Then he throws the bones and fat into the altar fire for the god (who consumes it by inhaling the smoke that rises into the sky). The rest of the animal is cooked and eaten by the worshipers.

During the sacrifice, the priest keeps his head covered with his toga and musicians play, rituals intended to ward off the

During a sacrifice, a group of priests examines a bull's internal organs. If there is something odd about them, it may be a bad omen, in which case the sacrifice is invalid.

sights or sounds of bad omens, such as birds alighting in unexpected places or priests finding strange growths or markings on the victim's organs. If such an omen does appear, the entire ritual has to be repeated. Indeed, it is extremely important to get all the steps of the ritual right because if any single detail is wrong, the god may refuse the sacrifice. (Sometimes plants are sacrificed instead of or in addition to animals. There are also liquid sacrifices, called libations, which most commonly consist of pouring wine, honey, or milk on the ground or over an altar.) These, then, are those essentials of the Roman religion that foreign visitors need to know to understand the worship that takes place on a daily basis in the capital city.

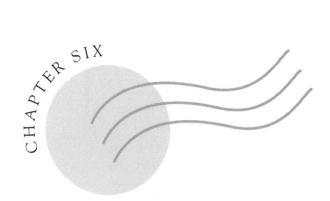

CHAPTER SIX

The Public Games

Without doubt, the city of Rome stages the greatest public spectacles in the known world. Though chariot races, gladiatorial combats, and wild animal fights are held in many parts of the Empire, none compare in sheer size and scope with those in the capital. For that reason, almost all those visiting the city try to attend at least one of the public games during their stay. And tourists who come from lands beyond the Empire's

A group of criminals meet their fate in a wild beast show staged in Rome's famous Colosseum.

Why the Romans Dislike Greek Sports

It is important to note that the Romans make a distinction between martial public games, particularly gladiatorial combats and wild animal fights, and Greek-style athletic contests. The latter encompass mainly Olympic-style events such as running, jumping, discus-throwing, and wrestling. Boxing and chariot racing are the only Greek sports the Romans really enjoy, and the Roman versions are considerably more vigorous and bloody. One reason the Romans have a disdain for Greek sports is that Greek athletes often train and compete in the nude. Most Romans reject this practice as effeminate (unmanly) and morally decadent. The famous first-century B.C. orator Cicero summed up the Roman view when he said that stripping in public is the beginning of evildoing. Another important difference between Greek and Roman sports involves the issue of citizen participation. The vast majority of Romans greatly enjoy watching large-scale, violent games, which they view as a form of entertainment; but for a Roman citizen actually to participate in such public spectacles is viewed as improper, undignified, and socially unacceptable. This view is completely contrary to that of Greek society, which encourages and glorifies athletic participation by citizens. The Roman attitude is undoubtedly motivated by pride. The Romans have always been a conservative, austere people who take special pride in their military prowess and consider losing in battle the ultimate disgrace. Simply put, for most Romans defeat in an athletic competition is too much like defeat in war.

borders are especially impressed, sometimes even amazed.

A Brief Background of the Games

A question often asked by foreign visitors who attend these games is how Rome came to stage such spectacular entertainments, which are rare, small-scale, or even nonexistent in their homelands. Of the various kinds of Roman public games, all but the gladiatorial fights are called *ludi*. Originally they were connected with various religious festivals; but by the late Republic they had become more secular in nature. Though chariot races and fights to the death between gladiators existed in the days of the kings and in early republican times, they were small-scale and staged infrequently (as well as privately funded in the case of gladiatorial combats). Not until the late Republic and early Empire did these and other spectacles become large-scale institutions sponsored solely by the government.

As public games became increasingly popular, the government made them part of a twofold policy designed to cater to the

The magnificent Circus Maximus, the largest racetrack in the world. Here, hundreds of thousands of spectators watch thrilling displays of skill and courage.

people's wants and needs (and also to help maintain order). First, public officials sponsor regular large-scale distributions of bread and other foodstuffs to the poor. As often witnessed by visiting merchants and tourists, about 150,000 urban Romans receive such handouts at hundreds of distribution centers located across the capital. Senators, military generals, and the emperors also spend huge sums subsidizing public festivals, shows, and games. This policy of appeasing the masses through both free food and entertainment has come to be called "bread and circuses" (*panem et circenses*), after a recent sarcastic remark by the popular humorist Juvenal. "There's only two things that concern the masses," he said, "bread and circus games."[17] An even more recent and more revealing description is that of Marcus Cornelius Fronto, the greatest Roman orator of our age. According to Fronto, the emperor Trajan, who reigned from 98 to 117, had such a shrewd understanding of political science that he

gave his attention even to actors and other performers on stage or on the race track or in the arena, since he knew that the Roman people are held in control principally by two things— free grain and shows—that political support depends as much on the entertainments as on matters of serious import, that neglect of serious problems does the greater harm, but neglect of entertainments brings damaging unpopularity, that gifts [from the emperor] are less eagerly and ardently longed for than shows, and finally, that gifts placate [appease] only the common people on the grain dole, singly and individually, but the shows placate everyone.[18]

One of Rome's Most Popular Tourist Sights

Of the public shows mentioned by Juvenal and Fronto, perhaps the most popular of all, with locals and visitors alike, are the chariot races (*ludi circenses*), held in the mighty Circus Maximus. One of the most popular tourist sights in the entire Roman Empire, this immense racetrack is more than a third of a mile long and 450 feet wide and occupies almost the entire valley between the Palatine and Aventine Hills.

The facility's seating can accommodate about 150,000 spectators, and another 100,000 or so crowd the nearby hillsides during the races (which normally number twenty-four per day).

These fans are typically a liberal mix of men, women, freedmen, and slaves; anyone who can find a place to sit or stand can attend. Admission is free. Because they tend to watch for many hours at a stretch, the spectators often sit on cushions, either carried from home or rented at the circus. Many also snack on food brought from home or bought from vendors and snack bars located beneath the stands.

Tourists are warned to be cautious when milling about in these great crowds, as pickpockets, prostitutes, and other unsavory characters regularly ply their trades in the circus. Visitors should also note that these spectacles are so huge and expensive to stage that they are held in Rome on only seventeen or eighteen days

Although chariot races are the usual fare, occasionally one can see footraces like this one in the Great Circus.

One charioteer attempts to cut off his opponent as the two approach one of the turns. It is not unusual to see one or more vehicles crash in the average race.

each year. So those desiring to attend should find out the dates and plan ahead accordingly.

For those visitors who have never been to Rome before, attending the chariot races in the Great Circus affords the opportunity to see in person some of the most famous athletes in the world; many of the most popular of the charioteers, who are household names from one end of the Mediterranean to the other, race only in the capital. Because their wide fan following includes many of the tourists who visit Rome each year, some helpful information about these drivers and their vehicles is provided.

First, some charioteers become not only renowned but wealthy as well, even though most of them begin as slaves or poor commoners. Although the owners of the horses receive the purse money, they pay their drivers; and successful charioteers eventually gain their freedom (if they started out as slaves) and begin receiving hefty percentages of the purse. This situation prompted Juvenal to remark, "You'll find that a hundred lawyers scarcely make more than one successful jockey."[19] How successful can a racer become? One of the more popular charioteers, Calpurnianus, won 1,127 victories, including several that he claims paid him 40,000 *sesterces* (about forty times the annual wage of an average Roman soldier) or more. Another popular charioteer, Crescens, began racing at age thirteen and died at age twenty-four, earning more than 1.5 million *sesterces* in his short but glorious career.

Various kinds of chariots are driven by these men. The most common are the four-horse versions, called *quadrigae*, while the two-horse versions, the *bigae*, are seen fairly often. Less frequently seen, although not rare, are races for vehicles with three horses (*trigae*), six (*seiuges*), eight (*octoiuges*), and even ten (*decemiuges*). Another race staged only occasionally is the *pedibus ad quadrigam*, in which two men stand in a chariot; when the vehicle crosses the finish line, one of them jumps out and sprints once around the course. In addition, the crowds enjoy the antics of the *desultorii*, who entertain in the intervals between the chariot races. More of an acrobat than a rider, a *desultor* stands on the backs of two horses that are reined together and performs various stunts and tricks.

The charioteers are supported by various rival racing organizations, or factions (*factiones*), one of the more important social, as well economic, aspects of the races. A *factio* is a private stable run by a businessman, a *dominus factionis*, who hires out his horses, equipment, and drivers (many of whom are slaves and therefore his property) to the government magistrate who finances and supervises the races. The *domini factionum* can and often do grow rich from collecting not only their rental fees, but also the often considerable prize money for winning races.

Each faction is identified by the color of the tunics worn by its drivers. The four traditional colors—the whites, reds, blues, and greens—are very ancient, dating back to the days of the kings. (There were no factions in that early period. What seems to have happened is that the drivers wearing these colors became fan favorites, prompting the perpetuation of loyal fan support for the colors; over time the rivalry between the four colors became fierce. And later, when actual racing organizations emerged about a hundred years ago, each fan-following came to identify itself with a faction and vice versa.)

Thrills and Spills on the Track

A day of chariot racing in the Great Circus begins with a *pompa*, a colorful parade that winds its way through the heart of the city. It begins on the Capitoline Hill, moves down into and through the Forum, then goes along the western base of the Palatine Hill until it reaches the Circus Maximus. Leading the way is the games magistrate, who rides in a magnificently decorated chariot, wears a purple toga, and holds an ivory scepter topped by an eagle (symbol of Rome). At his sides and behind him are hundreds of young men decked out in their finest clothes. And behind them come the chariots, followed by various priests and public officials.

When the parade ends and it is time for the first race to commence, four drivers (each usually, though not always, representing one of the four traditional colors) undergo a lottery to determine their starting positions. Then the race begins. The charioteers have to complete seven full laps (about two and a

Two drivers fight for the lead in this exciting race. The chariot on the inside lane will gain ground in the next lap and end up winning the contest.

half miles), during which time they desperately and ruthlessly vie for every possible advantage. Each attempts to maneuver into the inside lane, against the racetrack's central spine (the *euripus*), because the distance of a lap in this position is somewhat shorter than in the outer lanes.

Often, the men try to sabotage one another by breaking a rival's wheels or axles or by other nefarious means. The most spectacular result of such on-track warfare is the "shipwreck" (*naufragium*), in which a chariot and its horses crash into a mass of twisted debris and broken bones. Such suspense, danger, violence,

blood-spilling, and death is undoubtedly what draws and satisfies the crowds.

Indeed, finding a Roman who does not enjoy the races would be difficult. A rare exception was that famous letter writer Pliny the Younger, who died about thirty years ago. He held himself intellectually above what he called the "childish passions" of the racing scene, saying:

If they [the fans] were attracted by the speed of the horses or the drivers' skill one could account for it, but in fact it is the racing-colors they really support and care about, and if the colors were to be exchanged in mid-course during

a race, they would transfer their favor and enthusiasm and rapidly desert the famous drivers and horses whose names they shout as they recognize them from afar. Such is the popularity of a worthless shirt. . . . When I think of how this futile, tedious, monotonous business can keep them sitting endlessly in their seats, I take pleasure in the fact that their pleasure is not mine.[20]

Gladiators and the World-Famous Colosseum

As locals and tourists alike can attest, next to the chariot races the most popular games in Rome are the gladiatorial combats (*munera*) and wild animal fights staged in the Empire's greatest amphitheater—the Colosseum. Perhaps *the* most popular tourist attraction in the known world, it is located in a natural depression in the valley between the Caelian and Esquiline Hills, directly across the street from the Baths of Titus. Completed in A.D. 81 by Domitian, it is the largest amphitheater in the Empire; its great oval bowl measures 620 by 513 feet, it towers to a height of 156 feet, and it seats some fifty thousand people.

As for the bloody fights staged in the Colosseum, the Romans borrowed the custom of the *munera* from the Etruscans, who once dominated the region north of the city. The Etruscans believed that when an important man died, his spirit required a blood sacrifice to survive in the afterlife (hence the literal translation of *munera*: "offerings" or "obligations" to the dead). So outside these individuals' tombs they staged rituals in which warriors fought to the death.

In Rome, the *munera* were at first relatively small, private affairs funded and staged by aristocrats. Over time, however, both they and the general populace came to view these games more as entertainment than funeral ritual, and demand grew for making gladiator bouts part of the public games. Julius Caesar was the first leader to stage large-scale public *munera*, presenting 320 pairs of gladiators in 65 B.C.

Among the most often asked questions by foreigners visiting Rome and attending the Colosseum spectacles are:

Who are these men who fight to the death? and why do they do it? The answer to the first question is that they are mostly prisoners, slaves, and criminals who train long and hard in special schools. A few are free, paid volunteers. They do it if they have financial difficulties since there is generous prize money for the winners. They may also do it if they are motivated by the physical challenge and appeal of danger, or at the prospect of becoming popular idols and sex symbols who can have their pick of pretty young girls.

Foreign visitors also tend to be confused at first by the different types and categories of gladiator. One of the four main types is the heavily armed Samnite (also called a *hoplomachus* or *secutor*). He carries a sword or a lance, a *scutum* (the rectangular shield used by Roman legionary soldiers), a metal helmet, and protective armor on his right arm and left leg. Another type, the Thracian, is less elaborately armed. He wields a curved short sword, the *sica,* and a small round shield, the *parma.* A third kind of gladia-

tor, the "*murmillo,*" or "fishman" (after the fish-shaped crest on his helmet) is similar to a Samnite, but less heavily armed. A *murmillo* customarily fights still another kind of warrior, the *retiarius,* or "net-man," who wears no armor at all. A *retiarius* attempts to ensnare his opponent in his net and then to stab him with a long, razor-sharp trident (a three-pronged spear). Besides the pairings of these main gladiator types, there are a number of special and offbeat types and pairings. These include *equites,* who fight on horseback using lances, swords, and/or lassoes; the *essedarii,* who confront each other on chariots; and the *andabatae,* who grapple while blindfolded by massive helmets with no eyeholes.

On a day when these men are scheduled to fight, they first enter the arena in a colorful parade. Then they draw lots to decide who will fight whom, and an official inspects their weapons to make sure they are sound and well-sharpened. Finally, the gladiators soberly raise their weapons toward the highest ranking offi-

A cutaway drawing of the Colosseum reveals its circular rows of arches. The structure draws thousands of visitors from around the world each year.

Most of the time gladiators face off one on one. However, on occasion large groups fight, as shown here. The men first draw lots to see who will fight whom.

cial present (usually either the emperor or games magistrate) and recite the phrase, "We who are about to die salute you!"

After that, the first pairing begins. Having no rules or referees, the combat is sometimes desperate and often savage. It frequently ends with the death of one of the contestants; but some matches are declared a draw. Another common outcome is when one gladiator goes down

65

A downed gladiator appeals to the spectators to spare his life. However, they are not in the mood to do so on this occasion, so he is a doomed man.

wounded. He is allowed to raise one finger, a sign of appeal for mercy, after which the emperor or magistrate decides his fate, usually in accordance with the crowd's wishes.

Animal Fights and Acts

Another large-scale arena attraction very popular with tourists are ferocious fights between humans and beasts and between beasts and beasts. Generally termed *venationes*, or "hunts," they were originally minor spectacles presented mainly in early morning before the bulk of spectators had

arrived. By the early years of the Empire, however, the hunts had become popular enough to warrant staging them in late afternoon, when more people attend arena shows.

The government imports animals from the far reaches of its realm, and often beyond, including tigers, leopards, lions, bulls, elephants, ostriches, and crocodiles. In some spectacles they engage in mortal combat with a "hunter" (*venator*), who wields a spear, sword, club, bow and arrow, or some other weapon. The number of animals killed in this manner is quite large at times. More than 9,000 beasts died in 100 days during Titus's reign; and when Trajan presented immense spectacles lasting 123 days in A.D. 107, at least 11,000 animals met their deaths.

Not all of the beasts that enter the arena are killed, however. A wild animal show in the Colosseum usually concludes with some trained animal acts that audiences always find delightful

A venator narrowly escapes death as a lion seizes his horse. The wild beast hunts are exciting in large part because they are so dangerous for both the animals and men.

A Passion for Gambling

Though the Romans love their public games, they have just as fervent a passion for another form of entertainment—gambling. Roman gambling was so prevalent in republican times that laws were passed against it; the penalty for engaging in betting (*sponsiones*), for example, was a fine amounting to four times the value of the stakes. The emperors have maintained these prohibitions. However, there are exceptions and loopholes. Gambling is acceptable during the popular Saturnalia festival in December, for instance, and betting on public games such as chariot races and gladiatorial combats is allowed. In any case, laws against gambling are difficult to enforce and only rarely invoked. The fact is that huge amounts of money are wagered on horse and chariot races, dice games, and numerous other games. "When was gambling more frantic than it is today?" Juvenal quipped a few years ago in one of his satires. "Is it not plain lunacy to lose ten thousand on the turn of the dice, yet not have a shirt to give your shivering slave?" Besides betting on sporting events, the most popular games of chance involve coins, dice (*tesserae*), pebbles, pieces of bone, and other tokens. One common game is "heads or tails" (*capita et navia*), in which the gamblers try to guess the outcomes of coin tosses. There is also "odd or even" (*par impar*), in which a player hides some pebbles, nuts, or other tokens in his hand and his opponent has to guess how many he holds. A variation of odd or even is *micatio*, in which two players repeatedly raise random numbers of fingers and simultaneously guess how many until one guesses right and wins the wager.

and/or fascinating. Among these are monkeys, who are often dressed as soldiers and drive miniature chariots drawn by goats; lions that hold rabbits or even mice in their jaws without harming them; and bears that climb poles and play ball. In short, the games presented in the Colosseum have something for nearly all tastes. No wonder they are so popular!

CHAPTER SEVEN

Sightseeing in Rome

The city of Rome features some of the most important and famous religious and political monuments and institutions in the known world. Among them are enormous games facilities like the Circus Maximus and Colosseum; grand and magnificent temples to Jupiter, Apollo, Mars, and numerous other gods; the Senate House and other government buildings; mammoth bathhouses that accommodate thousands of people at once; not to mention

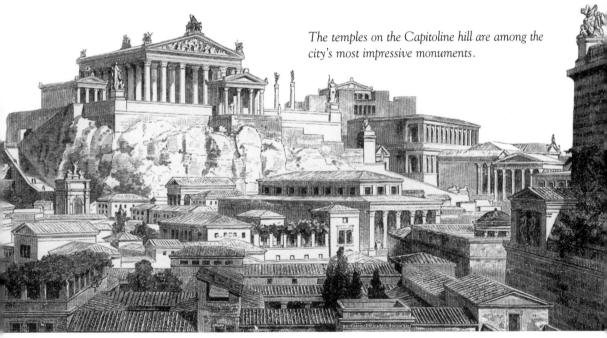

The temples on the Capitoline hill are among the city's most impressive monuments.

Augustus's Works, in His Own Words

Augustus was the greatest builder in Roman history. In this excerpt from his autobiography, the Res gestae, *he lists only a few of the construction projects he sponsored.*

I built the following structures: the Temple of Apollo on the Palatine with its porticoes [porches]; the Temple of the Deified Julius [Caesar] . . . the portico at the Circus Flaminius . . . the state box at the Circus Maximus; the temples of Jupiter the Smiter and Jupiter the Thunderer on the Capitoline . . . the temples of Minerva and Queen Juno and of Jupiter Freedom on the Aventine. . . . I repaired the Capitol and the Theater of Pompey with enormous expenditures on both works, without having my name inscribed on them. I repaired the conduits of the aqueducts which were falling into ruin. . . . I repaired eighty-two temples of the gods in the city . . . neglecting none which at that time required repair. . . . On my own private land I built the Temple of Mars Ultor and the Augustan Forum from spoils of war. On ground bought for the most part from private owners, I built the theater adjoining the Temple of Apollo which was to be inscribed with the name of my son-in-law [and nephew] Marcus Marcellus [who died prematurely].

palaces, libraries, law courts, memorial pillars and victory arches, theaters, imperial tombs, and much more. Even if the only reason a visitor came to the city was to see such attractions, there are enough to keep him or her busy for several weeks. The sites listed below constitute only some of the major highlights, beginning in the Campus Martius, the large region west of the Capitoline and Quirinal Hills.

Augustus's Monuments in the Campus Martius

The Campus Martius is so crowded with monuments, temples, and other structures, it is difficult to imagine that less than two hundred years ago it was almost all open space. Among the prodigious builders who developed the area was the divine Augustus. Situated in the Campus's northern sector is his magnificent Ara Pacis (Altar of Peace), seen by many as the crowning artistic masterpiece of the Augustan Age (his fruitful forty-five-year reign). Erected in January 9 B.C., it is a monument to the era of peace, still ongoing, he initiated following the devastating civil wars. Leading magistrates, state priests, and the Vestal Virgins sometimes perform sacrifices beside it.

Made of blocks of travertine (a creamy-white variety of limestone) and marble, the altar is U-shaped, with its open end facing west and accessed by a staircase. A marble wall about 30 feet square and 16 feet high encloses the structure. On the outside of the east wall, facing the Via Flaminia (the main north-south route through the Campus), are beautiful relief sculptures, including one of the goddess Roma (divine spirit of the capital city) sitting atop a pile of armor between Honos and Virtus (the spirits of honor and virtue). Also prominent is a sculpture of Pax (goddess of peace). The north and south wall exteriors feature horizontal bands of sculptures containing more than one hundred human figures, including Augustus himself (who walks at the head of a procession that includes priests), his wife, Livia, and his associate and son-in-law, Marcus Agrippa.

Right beside the Ara Pacis is the large circular paved area that constitutes the base of the gigantic sundial Augustus bestowed on the Roman people in 10 B.C. An obelisk about 100 hundred feet high serves as the vertical pointer that casts a long shadow across the paving stones. Pliny the Elder provided this excellent description:

> Augustus used the obelisk in the Campus Martius in a remarkable way—namely to cast a shadow and thus mark the length of the days and nights. A paved area was laid out . . . in such a way that the shadow at noon on the shortest day might

This is the staircase on the open western side of the Altar of Peace, the wonderful monument erected by Augustus in 9 B.C. in the Campus Martius.

extend to the edge of the paving. As the shadow gradually grew shorter and longer again, it was measured by bronze rods fixed in the paving. . . . [The designer] placed a gold-plated ball on the apex of the monolith so that the shadow would be concentrated at its tip; otherwise the shadow cast would have been very indistinct. He got this idea, so it is said, from seeing the shadow cast by a man's head.[21]

Another magnificent structure erected by Augustus is the Theater of Marcellus, located on the far southern edge of the Campus, beside the Capitoline Hill and directly facing Tiber Island. The building was named after Augustus's beloved nephew, who died prematurely a few years before its dedication in 13 B.C. With seating for up to twenty thousand people, it is the largest theater in Rome

and has served ever since as the model for theaters erected accross the Empire. Having the shape of a hemisphere, like half a pie, the building's curved wall encloses rising tiers of seats, while its straight back wall, elegantly decorated on the side facing the audience, provides a backdrop for the semicircular stage.

To support the theater's heavy stone superstructure and seating, the builders employed two of the three most important basic hallmarks of Roman construction—the arch and the vault. A typical Roman arch begins with two vertical supports, called piers. Curving inward from the top of each pier is an arc of wedge-shaped stones, known as voussoirs (voo-SWARS), which meet the other arc at the central keystone at the top. A Roman vault is a three-dimensional version of an arch—in effect, a curved ceiling. The Theater of Marcellus features elegant-looking arcades

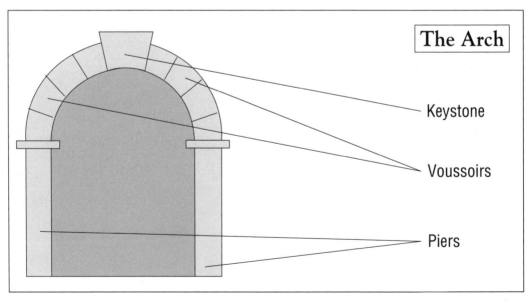

The Arch

Keystone

Voussoirs

Piers

The Pantheon, which stands on the Campus Martius, is one of the greatest examples of Roman architecture and building construction.

(rows of arches) on the outside wall, each of which opens into a barrel vault, a corridor with a curved ceiling running along its length. These corridors fan outward from the center like wheel spokes, incorporating an ingenious system of ascending ramps and entrances and exits for the spectators.

Augustus endeavored to leave his mark in the Campus Martius even after his death. In 28 B.C., he erected his own tomb, which became known as the Mausoleum of Augustus, on the bank of the Tiber about 1,100 feet to the northwest of the Ara Pacis. The Mausoleum is a circular structure with a main dome 300 feet in diameter and about 150 feet high; these impressive dimensions make it the largest tomb in the empire. (Out of respect for his illustrious predecessor, Hadrian was careful not to surpass these dimensions in erecting his own tomb on the opposite bank of the Tiber.)

The Noble Pantheon

The Campus Martius is also the site of one of the greatest examples of Roman architecture and construction—the Pantheon. Situated almost directly in the center of the Campus, it was erected between A.D. 118 and 125 by the emperor Hadrian. Actually, it is the third version of the building, the first having been built more

On entering the Pantheon, visitors will immediately notice its immense size. The dome is said to be the largest ever built in the known world.

than a century before by Augustus's friend and son-in-law, Agrippa. (The features and function of Agrippa's version were obliterated by later construction on the site; however, Agrippa's name still appears in a large inscription on the front of the building.) The name "Pantheon" combines the Greek words *pan*, meaning "all," and *theos*, meaning "god," based on the fact that it contains statues of all the gods.

Structurally speaking, the Pantheon consists of two main sections: a porchlike facade in the style of a Greco-Roman temple, and behind it a large spherical rotunda topped by a massive dome. The interior diameter of the rotunda, including the base of the dome, measures 150 feet. The walls and dome are composed of high-quality Roman concrete, and the whole building rests on a foundation of dense concrete some 15 feet deep. Inside the immense main hall, the building has an elegant, noble look and can also be very atmospheric when the light is right. Everyone agrees that the Pantheon is not to be missed.

Trajan's Forum

Moving out of the Campus Martius toward the east, skirting the northern edge of the Capitoline Hill, one runs into a series of impressive imperial fora, including (from east to west) the Forum of Trajan, the Forum of Augustus, and the Forum of Caesar. The newest of the group, the Forum of Trajan, was completed about A.D. 115. A true architectural masterpiece, its designer was Apollodorus of Damascus, an accomplished military engineer who built a bridge across the Danube River for Trajan when that emperor was campaigning in southern Germany in 106. A magnificent gateway leads from the Forum of Augustus into Trajan's forum. The latter is a huge open square bordered on the north by Trajan's markets and on the east and south by long, raised porches whose roofs are supported by rows of columns, all constructed of fine Numidian yellow marble. Several recessed niches contain beautiful larger-than-life-size statues.

The western end of the forum is demarcated and dominated by the Basilica Ulpia, an enormous rectangular structure containing law courts. The largest basilica in the Roman world, it is 600 feet long and 200 feet wide. The interior features aisles running along the sides, flanking a column-lined nave (central open area) two stories high; the columns in the lower colonnade are 36 feet high and made of gray Egyptian granite, while those in the upper colonnade are 30 feet high and made of Carystian green marble. The floor of the nave features a mixture of three marbles: Numidian yellow, Phrygian purple, and Lucullan red/black.

Exiting the basilica's western doors, one enters a large, picturesque courtyard in the center of which stands one of Rome's most imposing monuments—Trajan's Column. Erected in 113, the circular shaft rises to a height of 128 feet, not counting

Trajan's great commemorative column rises on one end of his magnificent forum.

the 16-foot-tall bronze statue of Trajan standing on top.[22] Tourists and local Romans alike marvel at the 600-foot-long sculpted frieze that winds in a spiral around the column's exterior. The frieze contains 155 separate scenes, more than 2,600 human figures, and tells the story of Trajan's campaigns in southern Germany. The interior of the column features a spiral staircase leading up to an observation platform from which one can enjoy a splendid panorama of the city.

On the north and south sides of the courtyard are Trajan's libraries. These marvelous repositories of knowledge are identical structures that neatly frame the great column. One contains books and documents in Latin, the other in Greek. Like the adjoining basilica, each is two stories high with a large open central area, although the libraries are considerably smaller, measuring about 86 by 63 feet. Large tables and numerous chairs are provided for both scholars and everyday readers to wile away a pleasant hour or an entire day. There is certainly enough material to keep one busy for a long time; each library has an estimated ten thousand scrolls. (For the benefit of foreigners from lands where books are not nearly so plentiful, Greek and Roman books are written in black ink on sheets of papyrus, a parchment made from a water plant that grows in abundance in

The First Roman Libraries

Many of the more educated visitors to Rome enjoy spending some leisure time at one of the city's fine libraries. Before the Romans established libraries, the Greeks had them, the largest and most renowned being the one at Alexandria, Egypt, containing, it is said, seven hundred thousand volumes (in the form of papyrus rolls). Other large Greek libraries still exist at Pergamum and Athens. It was collections of Greek books taken back to Italy by Roman generals and administrators that formed the nucleus of the first Roman libraries. The first private Roman collection, for example, was the one Lucius Aemilius Paullus seized from the Macedonian king Perseus in 168 B.C. Beginning in the first century B.C., private libraries became fairly common in Rome and other Italian towns. (Herculaneum had a library containing almost two thousand scrolls before it was destroyed by the eruption of Mount Vesuvius in A.D. 79.) Rome's first public library was created by the historian and literary patron Gaius Asinius Pollio during Augustus's reign. Augustus himself established a library in the Campus Martius and another on the Palatine Hill. Among the finest of Roman libraries are those erected by Trajan in his forum in the early years of this century, one featuring manuscripts in Greek, the other in Latin.

A scholar studies some scrolls in one of the many small libraries found in Rome. A few libraries are much larger, including those built by the emperor Trajan.

Egypt. The sheets are pasted together, producing a much longer sheet, usually about 30 feet long. This sheet is rolled up around a wooden stick; and the resulting scroll is easy both to store and to unroll for reading.)

The Forum of Augustus

Directly adjoining the Forum of Trajan in the east is the Forum of Augustus, begun in 25 B.C. and completed and dedicated in 2 B.C. Several years before, when he was still called Octavian, Augustus had promised that if victorious against Caesar's assassins, he would give thanks by build-ing a temple to Mars. The Forum of Augustus contains the fulfillment of that oath—the Temple of Mars Ultor, flanked by two long and quite stunning colonnaded walkways.

Augustus himself recalled this achievement rather briefly and modestly in his *Res gestae*, the autobiography he left to the Roman people. "On my own private land," he said, "I built the temple of Mars Ultor and the Augustan Forum from spoils of war."[23] Yet this structure is anything but modest. The front of the temple features eight Corinthian columns, each

The splendor of Rome's main square, the Forum Romanum, draws tourists from across the Empire. A sacrifice, in progress in front of the Temple of Castor (left), is one of many public spectacles held here.

an incredible 60 feet high. (The three Greco-Roman architectural orders are defined by the design of their column capitals, or tops. The simplest order is the Doric, with capitals made up of plain stone slabs; the Ionic order features capitals with decorative scrolls; and the most ornate, the Corinthian, has capitals covered by masonry leaves.) Eight more identical columns run down each side. In A.D. 19, Augustus's successor, Tiberius, added the two triumphal arches that rise on either side of the temple.

Inside the temple, in the main room (*cella*), the floors are paved with alternating strips of yellow, purple, and red/black marble. And marble colonnades and statues abound, creating an atmosphere of extreme elegance. Among the highlights are three large statues—of the war god Mars in full armor, the love goddess Venus (with her attendant Cupid), and Augustus's adoptive father, Julius Caesar. The room also houses Caesar's sword, which remains one of the city's more popular tourist attractions.

The Main Forum

Moving southward from the region of the imperial fora, one soon comes to the city's principal forum—the Forum Romanum ("forum of Rome"), located in the basin situated between the Capitoline, Palatine, and Quirinal Hills. The area was originally marshy, with a stream running through it, and only after the stream bed was moved and the marshes drained late in the period of the Roman monarchy did large-scale building begin there.

In republican times, the open area in the center of the Forum became heavily lined by temples, basilicas, statues, and shops; and people gathered in the Comitium, an open area on the western end, to hear political speeches at various rostra (platforms for speakers). Julius Caesar, Augustus, and other wealthy individuals erected impressive public buildings in the main Forum, including the Basilica Aemilia (or Pauli), Basilica Julia, Temple of Castor and Pollux, Temple of Saturn, and Temple of Concord. The sight of so many magnificent buildings clustered close together, along with numerous towering memorial columns and huge marble statues, is positively breathtaking and inspires awe in all who see it.

Another important landmark is the Senate House (*Curia*), located near the northern end of the Forum. A number of versions existed on the site over the years, most of which burned down. Julius Caesar began work on the present one, and his adopted son Augustus finished it in 29 B.C. The front pediment (triangular gable beneath the sloping roof) contains a statue of the goddess Victory on a globe; and inside, another statue of Victory graces an altar on one end of the

main room. That chamber features three curved, stepped stone platforms, each holding chairs for the senators. Overall, the building is small in comparison to the grand structures surrounding it; and visitors often find it astonishing that for centuries decisions affecting the fate of the entire world were made within these modest walls.

The Forum of Caesar

This impressive forum was dedicated in 46 B.C. on a plot of land purchased by Julius Caesar just north of the Forum Romanum. It is rectangular in shape, with colonnades on three sides and a large decorative entranceway on the fourth. This forum features some shops but is dominated by the splendid Temple of Venus Genetrix ("Universal Mother"), the goddess from whom Caesar's family claimed descent. Caesar himself donated a large number of valuable art objects to the temple, including antique paintings, a collection of engraved jewels, a gold statue of his Egyptian lover (Cleopatra), and a string of British pearls. A fire later ravaged much of Caesar's forum; but the emperor Trajan restored it, rededicating it in A.D. 108.

Visiting the Baths of Trajan

Sightseeing in the fora and other areas in the heart of the city is exhilarating but also strenuous and exhausting, especially in the summer months. By the end of the day, therefore, the visitor is almost certainly ready for a relaxing bath, swim, and/or massage. Rome has many bathhouses (*thermae*), of course. But for those who have spent the day downtown, a visit to the Baths of Trajan is advised. The baths lie within walking distance of the fora; they are also the largest and most impressive baths in town and constitute a major tourist attraction in and of themselves. Designed by Apollodorus of Damascus (the same architect who did Trajan's forum) and completed in A.D. 109,

This vestibule from a local bathhouse is nearly identical to one in the town of Herculaneum, near Vesuvius in Campania. The water has temporarily been drained from the pool to allow for repairs.

The Secret of Hot Air and Water

Many foreign visitors to Rome, especially from less civilized areas (such as northern Europe), are astounded by the plentiful amounts of hot air and water in the public baths. The secret to such heating is an ingenious system called a hypocaust. Hollow spaces beneath the floors and often inside the walls of warm rooms lead to narrow, stone-lined tunnels beneath the building. These tunnels, in turn, lead to a large furnace located somewhere outside. Slaves keep the furnace fueled with wood or coal; and the heat generated passes through the system, warming the rooms inside. It is not all that mysterious and complicated, after all. But it *is* expensive to install such a system, so only the well-to-do can afford to heat their homes this way.

Trajan's baths are located about a third of a mile east of the Forum Romanum, just to the north of the Colosseum. The bathhouse itself is about 600 by 450 feet and is surrounded by gardens and walkways, the whole grounds covering a whopping 1,000 by 700 feet!

Like other large Roman baths, those of Trajan feature various hot and cold rooms, pools, saunas, and dressing rooms. Even the poor can afford to go often since the entrance fee is minimal (and children are admitted free). Separate facilities are provided for women (though people sometimes ignore the rules and engage in mixed bathing, which society frowns on but often winks at).

These baths, like other such facilities in Rome, are used for much more than just bathing, however. Either before, after, or instead of bathing, the visitor can enjoy many other pastimes, including exercise rooms where people stretch and lift weights; gyms where they play ball games, wrestle, and jog; restaurants and snack bars; and small libraries and reading rooms. In addition, the baths afford opportunities for social fellowship and the exchange of news and gossip.

At any given moment, therefore, hundreds or even thousands of people are engaged in dozens of different activities within the baths. So, needless to say, it can be very noisy, as emphasized by Seneca, the brilliant tutor of the emperor Nero. Seneca had an apartment situated directly above a public bathhouse, and in one of his surviving letters he tells a friend:

If silence is necessary . . . for someone who wants seclusion to read and study, then I'm really in trouble. Here I am surrounded on all sides by a variety of noises. . . . Just imagine the whole range of voices which can irritate my

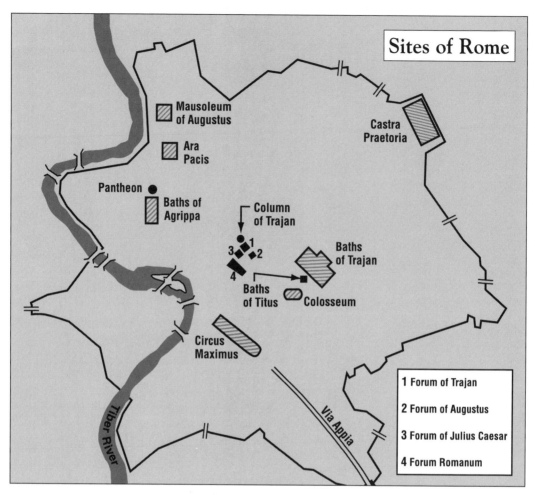

Sites of Rome

Mausoleum of Augustus

Ara Pacis

Castra Praetoria

Pantheon

Baths of Agrippa

Column of Trajan

Baths of Trajan

Baths of Titus

Colosseum

Circus Maximus

Tiber River

Via Appia

1 Forum of Trajan

2 Forum of Augustus

3 Forum of Julius Caesar

4 Forum Romanum

ears. When the more muscular types are exercising and swinging about lead weights in their hands . . . I hear groans. And when they hold their breath for a while and then let it out, I hear hissing and very hoarse gasps. . . . If a ballplayer comes along and begins to count his score aloud, I'm definitely finished. Imagine also a quarrelsome drunk, or sometimes a thief caught in the act, or a man who loves to sing in the bath. And then imagine people diving into the pool with a great splash of water.[24]

Noisy or not, regular visits to Trajan's baths or other large bathhouses are a must during anyone's stay in the teeming capital city.

CHAPTER EIGHT

Trips to Nearby Sites

Although visitors to Rome can busy themselves for weeks inspecting the city's many attractions, a number of sites lying in the general vicinity of the city are well worth seeing. These range from shrines to Rome's ancestors in the Latium plain; to the magnificent country villa of a former emperor; to the verdant, lovely fields of the world-famous Campania; to the awesome, spooky site where two bustling towns, including Pompeii, were destroyed by nature's wrath. All of the places described below are accessible by good roads and reachable within one to three days of travel by foot or wagon. Local guides are available at most of the sites for a small fee.

While en route to these sites, travelers from the provinces or foreign lands may well be surprised to find that they are not the only sightseers on the roads. Many Italians are perfectly familiar with the local attractions. Yet some, particularly members of the capital city's well-to-

do set, make a point of visiting the choicest sites over and over again. Perhaps this is because they do not have to work for a living (because their estates and investments supply them with ample incomes),

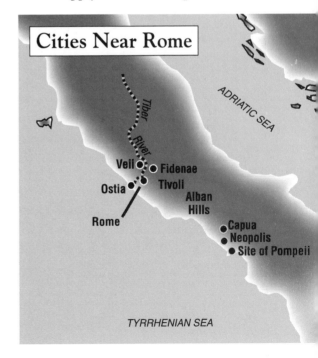

Cities Near Rome

are easily bored by mundane activities and therefore have little else to do, or because they prefer the quiet countryside over the noisy city. Whatever their motivations, Seneca summed up their situation with a touch of humor when he wrote that they

> undertake aimless journeys and wander up and down the coast. An unhealthy restlessness always afflicts them wherever they are, traveling by sea or by land. "Let's go to Campania." But luxury proves to be a bore. "Let's hurry to Bruttium and the woodlands of Lucania." Yet amidst these wild regions, they look for something refined so that they can relieve their delicate eyes of the unbroken desola-

tion of these uncultivated areas. . . . "No, let's go back to Rome." It's been much too long since their ears have heard thunderous applause.[25]

The Port of Ostia

Regular tourists are rarely bothered by the antics of these overprivileged few, and in fact more often view them affably as a touch of added local color. As for the places where they are most likely to meet up with them, one of the closest to the capital is Rome's port city of Ostia. (The most direct route from the capital is the Via Ostiensis, which leads westward to the coast.) According to tradition, King Ancus Marcius established the port in the seventh century B.C. Ostia has long regulated trade, collected customs dues, and

The view along the Italian coast as one approaches the port of Ostia is one of the most magnificent in the Mediterranean.

stored foodstuffs, particularly grain, for shipment upriver to Rome. During the Punic Wars (264–146 B.C.), Ostia also became an important naval base.

Travelers, including tourists and traders alike, will find Ostia a friendly town with many amenities. Among these are taverns, inns, bakeries, and numerous small shops selling food, clothes, and souvenirs. Also, befitting the cosmopolitan nature of a port that draws traders and travelers from across the known world, there are temples and shrines of all types; some cater to worshipers of the state gods, while Cybele, Isis, Serapis, Mithras (with fifteen shrines of his own), and other foreign gods are well represented. The port city also boasts a theater, built by Augustus's associate, Agrippa, which seats roughly three thousand spectators.

The Antiquities of Veii

From either Rome or Ostia, the traveler can find pleasant side trips both to the north and south. The region immediately to the north, the old Etruscan homeland of Etruria,[26] consists of lovely expanses of countryside green with natural vegetation, cultivated vines, and farmers' crops. One of the more rewarding stops is Veii, an old Etruscan stronghold that is now a small, quiet town perfect for those looking for a restful getaway from the city's hustle and bustle. Veii is located about nine miles north of Rome and about eighteen miles northeast of Ostia. From Rome, take the Via Flaminia for about two miles to the Via Cassia, which

This is one of the many old Etruscan tombs near Veii. Some say it is haunted.

proceeds northward. One will find Veii perched on a plateau just before the spot where the Via Clodia branches off toward the northwest.

For those fascinated by antiquities— that is, ancient ruins—Veii is a good bet. In the centuries that have elapsed since the Etruscan kingdoms were absorbed into the Roman commonwealth, many of the older Etruscan buildings have fallen into decay; and old Etruscan tombs, many containing fine statuary and paintings, dot the area. Some visitors say that these ancient places give them a feeling of nostalgia for past ages when true heroes lived. Others claim the ruins are haunted, though this may be only a story perpetuated by the locals to attract curious tourists.

Veii was one of the most powerful and splendid of the old Etruscan city-states. It is still an arresting site as one approaches it from the south.

Ghosts or not, tourists will find other things to do in Veii. Various structures in town have been rebuilt numerous times over the years; and several newer structures were added in the last two centuries, including a bathhouse, a small theater, and a *porticus* (market building containing merchants' stalls). The latter provides local wares and souvenirs for tourists from abroad as well as from other parts of Italy. Though definitely a Roman town now, Veii retains a certain ancient alien charm, as one can still find a few old locals who speak the old Etruscan language.

Quiet Fidenae

Also picturesque is the smaller, even quieter town of Fidenae, which is located about five miles southeast of Veii and five miles directly north of Rome. (From Rome, take the Via Salaria, which passes right through Fidenae.) Fidenae still attracts a number of tourists because it was the scene of a gruesome catastrophe—the collapse of a theater—a little more than a century ago. For a long time the town was fairly unimportant except as the site of periodic, privately sponsored public games staged in makeshift wooden amphitheaters. Luckily, most of the individuals who financed such structures were responsible enough to hire skilled architects and builders to ensure proper design and construction. But occasionally less reputable speculators trying to turn a fast profit hastily erected buildings that were poorly designed or that used substandard materials. Such shady practices led to the disastrous collapse, which occurred in A.D. 27. In his *Annals,* the distinguished Roman historian Tacitus recorded it, writing:

An ex-slave called Atilius started building an amphitheater at Fidenae for a gladiatorial show. But he neither rested its foundations on solid ground nor fastened the wooden superstructure securely. He had undertaken the project not because of great wealth or municipal ambition but for sordid profits. Lovers of such displays . . . flocked in—men and women of all ages. Their numbers, swollen by the town's proximity, intensified the tragedy. The packed structure collapsed, subsiding both inwards and outwards and . . . overwhelming a huge crowd of spectators and bystanders. Those killed at the outset of the catastrophe at least

escaped torture. . . . More pitiable were those, mangled but not yet dead, who knew their wives and children lay there too. In daytime they could see them, and at night they heard their screams and moans. . . . When the ruins began to be cleared, people rushed to embrace and kiss the corpses—and even quarreled over them, when features were unrecognizable but similarities of physique and age had caused wrong identifications. Fifty thousand people were mutilated or crushed in the disaster.[27]

Some visitors claim that on especially quiet days they can hear faint echoes of the victims' screams, though this may well be a fiction promoted by the locals to lure tourists to the town.

Hadrian's Villa

Another popular attraction in the region is Tivoli (or Tibur), located about eighteen miles northeast of Rome on the Via Tiburtina near a bend in the Anio River. Like Veii and Fidenae, early Tivoli fought

This drawing shows some of the lovely and imposing buildings at Hadrian's villa.

against the Romans until losing much of its surrounding territory to them (by 338 B.C.). Thereafter, the town became noted for its fine building stone (travertine) and its fruit orchards. But its main claim to fame is a series of luxurious villas, one used by Augustus, but the most splendid of all that of the present emperor's immediate predecessor, Hadrian, completed less than ten years ago.

Hadrian's villa, which many say is the largest and most beautiful in the known world, includes a palace, long, roofed walkways, gardens, bathhouses, and replicas of famous buildings from around the Mediterranean world. The latter represent the localities the emperor liked the most in his extensive travels. Many parts of the huge complex are not open to the public. But some visitors are allowed into the large building near the entrance—the Poikile. Modeled after the Stoa Poikile ("Painted Stoa") in Athens, one of Hadrian's favorite structures, it is a huge rectangle lined with columned walkways, with an immense swimming pool in the middle.

The Alban Hills

Though these northerly attractions make excellent day trips, the countryside south of Rome is just as inviting. Passing through the wide, pleasant Latium plain

The rolling Alban Hills, in the Plain of Latium, seen here, feature many lovely country villas, as well as numerous shrines dating back to Rome's early years.

(on either the Via Appia or Via Latina), one finds much rich farmland punctuated by some steep hills. The most prominent of these are the Alban Hills, which rise about twelve miles southeast of Rome. In the summer, the hillsides are cooler than the sweltering surrounding plain, so a number of country villas and resorts have grown up in the area. The hills also feature a number of shrines dating back to ancient times, when Rome was but one of many Latin towns in the region. Perhaps the most sacred and popular of these shrines is the sanctuary of Jupiter Latiaris, on the eastern side of the main hill, the Alban Mount.

Beneath the shrine, on the plain itself, is Alba Longa, a popular tourist spot. The ruins on the site are those of the ancient home town of Rome's founder, Romulus. Along with Lavinium, another small town with extensive ruins, located nearer the coast, Alba Longa played an important role in the events that gave rise to Rome and the Roman race itself. For the sake of foreigners who may be unfamiliar with this story, which any Roman schoolboy can recite in detail, said events are briefly as follows.

After fleeing the burning Troy (which the Greeks were sacking), a noble Trojan prince, Aeneas, made his way to Italy, landing at Cumae, on the southwestern coast. There, he sought out the Sibyl, a local prophetess. She told him he would not be able to fulfill his destiny (which the god Apollo had told him was to establish a kingdom in Italy) until he has fought a destructive war with the local inhabitants. Soon afterward, Aeneas and his followers landed at the mouth of the Tiber River and became embroiled in a war with the local Latins. After winning the conflict, Aeneas established the city of Lavinium, while his son, Ascanius, later founded Alba Longa closer to the Alban Hills. And from the union of the Trojan and Latin races, fulfilling the destiny ordained by Father Jupiter, sprang the lineage of the noble Romans, who today rule the known world. For the Romans, Jupiter had earlier told Venus, "I see no measure nor date, and I grant them dominion without end . . . the master race, the wearers of the toga. So it is willed!" [28]

Campania and the Ghosts of Pompeii

Continuing on southward from Latium, the traveler enters Campania, one of the most fertile and lushly green regions in all of Italy. Over the years, the rich volcanic soil and pleasant climate have attracted the wealthy and famous, many of whom have built stately villas, including some on the slopes of the volcano that dominates the area—Mount Vesuvius. The main towns are Capua, located about sixteen miles inland from the coast, and Neapolis, [29] on the shore of the picturesque Gulf of Cumae. [30]

Until about sixty years ago, two other important towns—Pompeii and Herculaneum—existed nearby, closer to the volcano. The famous giant eruption of A.D. 79 almost completely buried them, and each

A Brief Background of Capua

Capua is one of the principle cities of the region of Campania. Originally an Etruscan town, it came under Roman domination in the late fourth century B.C. and, thanks to its metalworking and other local industries, soon became one of Italy's wealthiest and most important cities. In 216 B.C., after Hannibal defeated the Romans at Cannae, the city switched to the Carthaginian side in the Second Punic War; but the Romans recaptured it in 211 B.C. and punished it by beheading its leaders, exiling most of the rest of the populace, and resettling it with new colonists. Today, Capua is one of the empire's most prominent and prosperous cities and is sometimes seen as the gateway to other parts of the lovely Campania.

year their sites draw many visitors who stop to pray or otherwise pay their respects to the thousands of victims lost.

Before the catastrophe, the larger of the two towns, Pompeii, was a thriving center with a population of some twenty thousand. It had the Roman realm's first stone amphitheater and was especially renowned for its many fine bakeries and restaurants, as well as its potent wine (said to cause severe hangovers). Herculaneum was a quieter resort town with several fine villas. Both places were badly damaged by an earthquake in A.D. 62 but quickly rebuilt, only to become, quite unexpectedly, the victims of Vesuvius's wrath a few years later.

Among the souvenirs available in Neapolis and nearby villages are pottery models of Vesusvius and plaques commemorating the lost towns. Also sold are copies of Pliny the Younger's published letters, one of which describes the erup-

tion in some detail (which turned out to be fortunate for later generations because, although many people witnessed the catastrophe, no one else wrote about it.) The letter is doubly fascinating because it records the demise of Pliny's uncle, the great scientist and writer Pliny the Elder, who bravely tried to study the disaster up close. In the opening of the letter, addressed to his friend the historian Tacitus, the younger Pliny thanks him for asking for a description of the elder Pliny's death so that he could "leave an accurate account of it for posterity." The letter continues:

My uncle was stationed at Misenum [a naval base on the northern edge of the Gulf of Cumae], in active command of the fleet. On 24 August, in the early afternoon, my mother drew his attention to a cloud of unusual size and appearance. . . . It was not clear at that distance from which mountain the cloud was rising (it was afterward known to be Vesuvius); its general appearance can best be expressed as being like an umbrella pine, for it rose to a great height on a sort of trunk and then split off into branches, I imagine because it was thrust upwards by the first blast and then left unsupported as the pressure subsided. . . . Sometimes it looked white, sometimes blotched and dirty. . . . My uncle . . . saw at once that it was important enough for a closer inspection, and he ordered a boat to be made ready. . . . [Pliny the

Elder crossed the bay, went ashore, and hurried to a friend's house.] Meanwhile on Mount Vesuvius broad sheets of fire and leaping flames blazed at several points, their bright glare emphasized by the darkness of night. . . . The buildings were now shaking with violent shocks, and seemed to be swaying to and fro as if they were torn from their foundations. . . . Elsewhere there was daylight by this time, but they [Pliny and his friends] were still in darkness, blacker and denser than any ordinary night. . . . [Reaching the beach, Pliny] suddenly collapsed, I imagine because the dense fumes choked his breathing. . . . When daylight returned on the 26th . . . his body

A quaint street scene in Pompeii shortly before Mt. Vesuvius destroyed the city.

The crater of Mt. Vesuvius looms above the towns lining the Gulf of Cumae. Before it destroyed Pompeii and Herculaneum, the mountain featured a tall conical peak.

was found intact and uninjured, still fully clothed and looking more like sleep than death. [31]

One can only guess how many more Romans lie in their own perpetual sleep beneath the new soil laid down by Vesuvius. What is more certain is that, like Rome's many past military heroes and statesmen, the ghosts of Pompeii and Herculaneum continue to beckon to people today, demanding that travelers take a moment and remember them and their sacrifices.

Notes

Chapter One: A Brief History of Rome

1. Aelius Aristides, *Roman Panegyric*, quoted in Naphtali Lewis and Meyer Reinhold, eds., *Roman Civilization, Sourcebook II: The Empire*. New York: Harper and Row, 1966, pp. 137–38.

2. Plutarch, *Life of Romulus*, in *Parallel Lives*, published complete as *Lives of the Noble Grecians and Romans*, trans. John Dryden. New York: Random House, 1932, p. 31.

3. This attitude derived partly from the widespread perception that the imperial government was too strong and entrenched to make any serious opposition viable. But more important, most Romans of the early Empire looked back on the late Republic as a period of death, destruction, and uncertainty; to avoid a repetition of such troubles, they were more than willing to accept a dictator as long as he was capable, fair, and maintained Rome's cherished beliefs and traditions.

4. Quoted in Suetonius, *The Twelve Caesars*, trans. Robert Graves, rev. Michael Grant. New York: Penguin Books, 1979, p. 69.

5. Quoted in Dio Cassius, *Roman History*, trans. Ernest Cary. Cambridge, MA: Harvard University Press, 1927, vol. 9, p. 64.

6. In fact, this optimism proved short-lived. Though Antoninus's successor, Marcus Aurelius, was himself a thoughtful, generous ruler, he had to contend with growing problems, including invaders on the northern borders; and the twelve-year reign of Aurelius's cruel and despotic son, Commodus (A.D. 180–192) marked the beginning of Rome's slow but steady decline.

Chapter 2: Weather and Physical Setting

7. Virgil, *Seventh Eclogue*, in *Works*, trans. James Rhoades, in Mortimer Adler, ed., *Great Books of the Western World*, vol. 13. Chicago: Encyclopaedia Britannica, 1952, pp. 22–23.

8. Actually, the name "Colosseum" was not coined for the building until early medieval times. The Romans called it the *Amphitheatrum Flavium*, or "Amphitheater of the Flavians," because its builders—Vespasian, Titus, and Domitian—belonged to the Flavian dynasty of emperors.

The term "Colosseum Valley" also developed later.

9. Juvenal, *Eleventh Satire* and *Fifth Satire*, in *Juvenal: The Sixteen Satires*, trans. Peter Green. New York: Penguin, 1974, pp. 228, 105.

Chapter 3: Transportation, Lodging, and Food

10. What are now France and Belgium.
11. Quoted in Lionel Casson, *Travel in the Ancient World*. Baltimore: Johns Hopkins University Press, 1994, p. 204.
12. The Latin term from which the modern word "itinerary" derives.

Chapter 4: Markets and Shopping

13. Aelius Aristides, *Roman Panegyric*, quoted in William G. Sinnegin, ed., *Sources in Western Civilization: Rome*. New York: The Free Press, 1965, p. 175.
14. An oily petroleum residue.
15. Pliny the Elder, *Natural History*, excerpted in *Pliny the Elder: Natural History: A Selection*, trans. John H. Healy. New York: Penguin Books, 1991, p. 286.

Chapter 5: Gods and Religious Festivals

16. After Christianity's rise, that faith converted the Saturnalia to Christmas; but most of the old customs were retained. The Christians converted other old Roman festivals as well, among them the Lupercalia, which became the Feast of the Purification of the Virgin Mary.

Chapter 6: The Public Games

17. Juvenal, *Tenth Satire*, in Green translation, p. 207.
18. Quoted in Jo-Ann Shelton, ed., *As the Romans Did: A Sourcebook in Roman Social History*. New York: Oxford University Press, 1988, p. 336.
19. Juvenal, *Seventh Satire*, in Green translation, p. 167.
20. Pliny the Younger, *Letters* 9.6, in *The Letters of the Younger Pliny*, trans. Betty Radice. New York: Penguin Books, 1969, p. 236.

Chapter 7: Sightseeing in Rome

21. Pliny the Elder, *Natural History*, p. 351.
22. The statue disappeared in medieval times and local Italians replaced it in 1588 with a statue of St. Peter, which is still in place.
23. Augustus Caesar, *Res gestae*, in Sinnegin, *Sources in Western Civilization: Rome*. p. 109.
24. Seneca, *Letter 56*, quoted in Shelton, *As the Romans Did*, p. 314.

Chapter 8: Trips to Nearby Sites

25. Quoted in Shelton, *As the Romans Did*, p. 331.
26. Modern Tuscany.
27. Tacitus, *The Annals*, published as *The Annals of Ancient Rome*, trans.

Raymond Chevallier, *Roman Roads*. Trans. N.H. Field. Berkeley: University of California Press, 1976. A scholarly, somewhat haphazardly organized volume that is, nonetheless, the most comprehensive single study of Roman roads and a tremendously valuable resource.

Amanda Claridge, *Rome: An Oxford Archaeological Guide*. New York: Oxford University Press, 1998. An excellent, highly informative guide to Rome's ancient sites, with numerous helpful maps and drawings. Highly recommended, especially for those contemplating an archaeological tour of Rome.

T.J. Cornell, *The Beginnings of Rome: Italy and Rome from the Bronze Age to the Punic Wars (c. 1000–264 B.C.)*. London: Routledge, 1995. This well-written, authoritative study of Rome's early centuries offers compelling arguments for rejecting certain long-held notions about these years, especially the idea that the Etruscans took over and ruled Rome. Very highly recommended.

F.R. Cowell, *Life in Ancient Rome*. New York: G.P. Putnam's Sons, 1961. Cowell, a noted expert on ancient Rome, here offers a commendable, easy-to-read study of most aspects of Roman daily life.

Michael Crawford, *The Roman Republic*. Cambridge, MA: Harvard University Press, 1993. This is one of the best available overviews of the Republic, offering various insights into the nature of the political, cultural, and intellectual forces that shaped the decisions of Roman leaders.

Jane F. Gardner, *Women in Roman Law and Society*. Indianapolis: Indiana University Press, 1986. An excellent study of women in Roman times. Highly recommended for those wishing to delve into some of the finer details of Roman life.

Michael Grant, *History of Rome*. New York: Scribner's, 1978. Comprehensive, insightful, and well written, this is one of the best available general overviews of Roman civilization from its founding to its fall.

———, *A Social History of Greece and Rome*. New York: Charles Scribner's Sons, 1992. Explores the ins and outs of ancient Roman social life and customs, including the role of women, rich versus poor, and the status of slaves and foreigners.

———, *The Visible Past: Recent Archaeological Discoveries of Greek and Roman History*. New York: Scribner's, 1990. An information-packed synopsis of notable archaeological methods and discoveries relating to the classical world.

John H. Humphrey, *Roman Circuses: Arenas for Chariot Racing*. Berkeley: University of California Press, 1986. This large, scholarly volume, the most comprehensive available study of the construction and use of Roman racing facilities, will appeal mainly to specialists in Roman history and culture.

Paul MacKendrick, *The Mute Stones Speak: The Story of Archaeology in Italy*. New York: St. Martin's Press, 1960. Though now somewhat dated, this book remains an important and informative summary of Italian archaeological methods and finds in the nineteenth and early twentieth centuries.

Colin O'Connor, *Roman Bridges*. Cambridge, UK: Cambridge University Press, 1993. The definitive modern source on Roman bridges, written by a noted bridge engineer who is also an excellent historian. Contains long, detailed sections on Roman roads, aqueducts, and the bridges that adorned them, along with appropriate photos and several useful lists and tables of statistics. Highly recommended for those interested in this subject.

Vera Olivova, *Sport and Games in the Ancient World*. New York: St. Martin's Press, 1984. This large, well-written volume begins with useful overviews of how experts think that sport originally evolved and early athletic practices in the Near East and Egypt. The author then examines Greek sports, beginning with the Bronze Age and Homeric depictions, and concludes with Etruscan games and Roman festivals and games.

Michael B. Poliakoff, *Combat Sports in the Ancient World*. New Haven, CT: Yale University Press, 1987. Detailed, well written, and well documented, this is the definitive recent study of ancient wrestling, boxing, pankration, and other combat sports.

L. Richardson Jr., *A New Topographical Dictionary of Ancient Rome*. Baltimore: Johns Hopkins University Press, 1992. The definitive recent scholarly study of ancient Roman sites.

Ancient Sources

Augustus Caesar, *Res gestae*, in William G. Sinnegin, ed., *Sources in Western Civilization: Rome*. New York: The Free Press, 1965.

Dio Cassius, *Roman History*. 9 vols. Trans. Ernest Cary. Cambridge, MA: Harvard University Press, 1927.

Marcus Cornelius Fronto, *Correspondence*. 2 vols. Trans. C.R. Haines. Cambridge, MA: Harvard University Press, 1965.

Juvenal, *Satires*, published as *The Sixteen Satires*. Trans. Peter Green. New York: Penguin, 1974.

Naphtali Lewis and Meyer Reinhold, eds., *Roman Civilization, Sourcebook II: The Empire*. New York: Harper and Row, 1966.

Livy, *The History of Rome from Its Foundation*. Books 1–5 published as *Livy: The Early History of Rome*. Trans. Aubrey de Sélincourt. New York: Penguin Books, 1971.

Pliny the Elder, *Natural History*. 10 vols. Trans. H. Rackham. Cambridge, MA: Harvard University Press, 1967; also excerpted in *Pliny the Elder: Natural History: A Selection*. Trans. John H. Healy. New York: Penguin Books, 1991.

Pliny the Younger, *Letters*, in *The Letters of the Younger Pliny*. Trans. Betty Radice. New York: Penguin Books, 1969.

Plutarch, *Parallel Lives*, published complete as *Lives of the Noble Grecians and Romans*. Trans. John Dryden. New York: Random House, 1932.

Jo-Ann Shelton, ed., *As the Romans Did: A Sourcebook in Roman Social History*. New York: Oxford University Press, 1988.

William G. Sinnegin, ed., *Sources in Western Civilization: Rome*. New York: The Free Press, 1965.

Suetonius, *The Twelve Caesars*. Trans. Robert Graves, rev. Michael Grant. New York: Penguin Books, 1979.

Tacitus, *The Annals*, published as *The Annals of Ancient Rome*. Trans. Michael Grant. New York: Penguin Books, 1989.

Virgil, *The Aeneid*. Trans. Patric Dickinson. New York: New American Library, 1961; also *Works*. Trans. James Rhoades, in Mortimer Adler, ed., *Great Books of the Western World*, vol. 13. Chicago: Encyclopaedia Britannica, 1952.

Additional Works Consulted

Lesley Adkins and Roy A. Adkins, *Handbook to Life in Ancient Rome*. New York: Facts On File, 1994.

Paul G. Bahn, ed., *The Cambridge Illustrated History of Archaeology*. New York: Cambridge University Press, 1996.

Anthony Birley, *Marcus Aurelius: A Biography*. New Haven, CT: Yale University Press, 1987.

Arthur E.R. Boak, *A History of Rome to 565 A.D.* New York: Macmillan, 1943.

S.F. Bonner, *Education in Ancient Rome from the Elder Cato to the Younger Pliny*. London: Methuen, 1977.

Keith R. Bradley, *Discovering the Roman Family: Studies in Roman Social History*. New York: Oxford University Press, 1991.

Matthew Bunson, *A Dictionary of the Roman Empire*. Oxford: Oxford University Press, 1991.

James H. Butler, *The Theater and Drama of Greece and Rome*. San Francisco: Chandler, 1972.

Alan Cameron, *Circus Factions: Blues and Greens at Rome and Byzantium*. London: Clarendon Press, 1976.

Gian B. Conte, *Latin Literature: A History*. Trans. Joseph B. Solodow, rev. Don P. Fowler and Glenn W. Most. Baltimore: Johns Hopkins University Press, 1999.

Tim Cornell and John Matthews, *Atlas of the Roman World*. New York: Facts On File, 1982.

L. Sprague de Camp, *The Ancient Engineers*. New York: Ballantine Books, 1963.

Joseph J. Deiss, *Herculaneum: Italy's Buried Treasure*. Malibu, CA: J. Paul Getty Museum, 1989.

Donald R. Dudley, *The Romans, 850 B.C.–A.D. 337*. New York: Knopf, 1970.

Florence Dupont, *Daily Life in Ancient Rome*. Oxford: Blackwell, 1989.

Elaine Fantham et al., *Women in the Classical World*. New York: Oxford University Press, 1994.

J. Ferguson, *The Religions of the Roman Empire*. London: Thames and Hudson, 1970.

John B. Firth, *Augustus Caesar and the Organization of the Empire of Rome*. Freeport, NY: Books for the Libraries Press, 1972.

Charles Freeman, *Egypt, Greece, and Rome: Civilizations of the Ancient Mediterranean*. Oxford: Oxford University Press, 1996.

Jane Gardner, *Roman Myths*. Austin: University of Texas Press and British Museum Press, 1993.

Michael Grant, *The Antonines: The Roman Empire in Transition*. London: Routledge, 1994.

———, *The Army of the Caesars*. New York: M. Evans, 1974.

———, *Gladiators*. New York: Delacorte Press, 1967.

———, *Myths of the Greeks and Romans*. New York: Penguin Books, 1962.

———, *The Roman Emperors*. New York: Barnes and Noble, 1997.

———, *The World of Rome*. New York: New American Library, 1960.

L.A. Hamey and J.A. Hamey, *The Roman Engineers*. Cambridge, UK: Cambridge University Press, 1981.

Edith Hamilton, *The Roman Way to Western Civilization*. New York: W.W. Norton, 1932.

John H. Humphrey, *Roman Circuses: Arenas for Chariot Racing*. Berkeley: University of California Press, 1986.

Ian Jenkins, *Greek and Roman Life*. Cambridge, MA: Harvard University Press, 1986.

Darcie C. Johnston, *Pompeii: The Vanished City*. Alexandria, VA: Time-Life Books, 1992.

Harold W. Johnston, *The Private Life of the Romans*. New York: Cooper Square, 1973.

Lawrence Keppie, *The Making of the Roman Army*. New York: Barnes and Noble, 1994.

Ellen Macnamara, *The Etruscans*. Cambridge, MA: Harvard University Press, 1991.

Harold Mattingly, *The Man in the Roman Street*. New York: W.W. Norton, 1966.

Alexander G. McKay, *Houses, Villas, and Palaces in the Roman World*. Baltimore: Johns Hopkins University Press, 1998.

Russell Meiggs, *Roman Ostia*. Oxford: Oxford University Press, 1973.

Meyer Reinhold, *Essentials of Greek and Roman Classics*. Great Neck, NY: Barron's Educational Series, 1960.

Chris Scarre, *Chronicle of the Roman Emperors*. New York: Thames and Hudson, 1995.

———, *Historical Atlas of Ancient Rome*. New York: Penguin Books, 1995.

John E. Stambough, *The Ancient Roman City*. Baltimore: Johns Hopkins University Press, 1988.

Chester G. Starr, *A History of the Ancient World*. New York: Oxford University Press, 1991.

J.M.C. Toynbee, *Death and Burial in the Roman World*. Baltimore: Johns Hopkins University Press, 1996.

Andrew Wallace-Hadrill, *Houses and Society in Pompeii and Herculaneum*. Princeton, NJ: Princeton University Press, 1994.

J.B. Ward-Perkins, *Roman Imperial Architecture*. New York: Penguin Books, 1981.

Mortimer Wheeler, *Roman Art and Architecture*. New York: Praeger, 1964.

K.D. White, *Roman Farming*. London: Thames and Hudson, 1970.

L.P. Wilkinson, *The Roman Experience*. Lanham, MD: University Press of America, 1974.

Fikret Yegül, *Baths and Bathing in Classical Antiquity*. Cambridge, MA: MIT Press, 1992.

Index

Picture Credits

About the Author

Historian Don Nardo has published many volumes about ancient Roman history and culture, including *The Decline and Fall of the Roman Empire*, *The Age of Augustus*, *Rulers of Ancient Rome*, *Life of a Roman Slave*, *Roman Roads and Aqueducts*, and Greenhaven Press's massive *Encyclopedia of Ancient Rome*. Mr. Nardo also writes screenplays and teleplays and composes music. Along with his wife, Christine, he resides in Massachusetts.